Outdoor Navigation with GPS

By Stephen W. Hinch

WILDERNESS PRESS · BERKELEY, CA

Outdoor Navigation with GPS

1st EDITION May 2004
2nd EDITION October 2007

Copyright © 2004 and 2007 by Stephen W. Hinch

Front cover photos copyright © 2007 by Stephen W. Hinch
Back cover photo copyright © 2007 by Stephen W. Hinch
Interior photos, except where noted, by Stephen W. Hinch
Maps & illustrations: Stephen W. Hinch
Cover & book design: Lisa Pletka
Book editor: Eva Dienel

ISBN 978-0-89997-445-3
UPC 7-19609-97445-1

Manufactured in the United States of America

Published by: **Wilderness Press**
 1200 5th Street
 Berkeley, CA 94710
 (800) 443-7227; FAX (510) 558-1696
 info@wildernesspress.com
 www.wildernesspress.com

Visit our website for a complete listing of our books and for ordering
information.

Cover photo: Yosemite Valley: N37° 43′ 03″ W119° 39′ 42″

SAFETY NOTICE: Although Wilderness Press and the author have made every
attempt to ensure that the information in this book is accurate at press time,
they are not responsible for any loss, damage, injury, or inconvenience that may
occur to anyone while using this book or the products mentioned in this book.
You are responsible for your own safety and health while in the wilderness. Be
aware that the products covered here may have been updated or changed since
this book was printed.

To Nicki, Juliana, and Greg

Acknowledgments

I'd like to thank the many people who helped me make this a better book. I first thank my wife, Nicki, who once again provided immense support throughout the entire project and proofread every page. She knows a lot about the subject and has been an invaluable assistant in helping the students in my GPS courses understand the concepts of outdoor navigation.

I would also like to thank Lincoln Turner and Joe Mehaffey, two people who provided valuable information for the first edition that continues to be important here. Lincoln's insight into traditional map-and-compass navigation has been especially valuable. Joe's wide knowledge of GPS, gained as co-owner of the website www.gpsinformation.net, also has been of immense help.

Roslyn Bullas and Eva Dienel, my editors at Wilderness Press, have been a pleasure to work with. Their suggestions and support have done a lot to improve the final book.

Finally, I would like to recognize those people within the industry whose help has been invaluable: Charlie Conley of DeLorme, Jessica Myers of Garmin, Steve Wegrzyn and Luke Morris of Lowrance, Michelle Wilkinson of National Geographic, Debby Chen of Magellan/Fleishman-Hillard, Bryan Roth of Groundspeak, Inc, and Walter Fishback of Revue Thommen AG.

Contents

Preface

Anyone who has ever purchased a GPS receiver and tried to read its instruction manual quickly makes a surprising discovery. Although each of the receiver's dozens of functions is described in glossy detail, you never quite learn how to employ them for anything useful, like actually navigating to a destination and returning safely.

You'd think that would worry GPS manufacturers. After all, newspaper headlines blaring, "Lost Hiker Found Dead Clutching GPS," don't do the industry any good. But you can't really blame the manufacturers. GPS is used in so many different ways, from hiking in the woods to navigating aircraft to coordinating artillery strikes, that it's just not practical for a single instruction manual to cover all these uses and more.

To fill the gap, a thriving cottage industry of aftermarket books, videos, and hands-on instructional classes has emerged. But even here, you are likely to walk away confused. Many books treat GPS as an end in itself rather than as simply one tool to help you navigate. If your goal is to learn how to use GPS to find your way in the outdoors, you don't need to confuse things by learning how to do such things as survey an archeological dig or dock a supertanker.

That's where this book comes in. It is written expressly for the outdoor navigator. You'll learn how to do the important things in a simple, easily understandable way. You'll see how to keep from getting lost, how to navigate both simple and complex routes, and how to use your GPS receiver in conjunction with those two other venerable tools of wilderness navigation, the map and compass. You won't be overwhelmed trying to understand the countless other GPS features you're unlikely to ever need.

Fortunately, when it comes to outdoor navigation, using a GPS receiver is not all that complicated. That's true whether you're a hunter returning to your pickup after a day in the woods, a backpacker on a multiday trek, or a geocacher searching for hidden treasures in a local park. Don't worry if the instruction manual that came with your receiver doesn't show you how to navigate. You'll learn that here.

Which brings me to the next important topic: As I've said, GPS is used in many different ways. The subject of this book is outdoor navigation. You'll see how to find your way in the outdoors but not how to navigate ships or aircraft. If you really want to use GPS to do something

TERMINOLOGY CLARIFICATION

Technically speaking, the term "GPS" describes the entire Global Positioning System. What you hold in your hand is a "GPS receiver." Lots of people just call it a "GPS," but I'll try to avoid that here. A slang term to describe a GPS receiver that's gained popularity in the geocaching community is "GPSr." It remains to be seen how widely it will be adopted, so I won't use it. If you want to understand the many other GPS-related terms, read the glossary at the back of the book.

dangerous like land an aircraft in a hailstorm or row solo across the Atlantic, you'll need expert instruction covering your specific needs.

There are dozens of different GPS receivers on the market today, and this book can't cover everything about all of them. Instead, this book will introduce the concepts of GPS navigation and illustrate them with the kinds of receivers used in the outdoors. That way, you'll be able to use what you learn regardless of which receiver you own today or which one you might buy next year.

Throughout this book, you'll see screen shots from a diversity of receivers from various manufacturers. Some are taken from receivers I own. Others come from ones manufacturers loaned to me expressly for this book. These screen shots can only serve as examples. It's not practical to explain the exact button sequences for every receiver out there. So don't throw away that instruction manual—you'll still need it. But the examples here should help you make more sense out of your own GPS unit.

No book can ever be a substitute for experience. Before you go charging off on that once-in-a-lifetime solo hike to the South Pole, get plenty of practice on lesser challenges. Spend some time using your receiver in the yard, around the neighborhood, in nearby parks—places where if you make a mistake, you won't need a search-and-rescue team to retrieve you. My strong words of advice are that until you are completely comfortable with GPS and can routinely navigate without making mistakes, don't use it to go anywhere you can't find your way back from without it.

Remember, a GPS receiver is a complex electronic instrument. While it's fairly rugged, it's not indestructible. Batteries can run down, it can get damaged from rough handling, or you can lose it off a 100-foot cliff. Before you start out on any serious wilderness exploration, make sure you carry a map and compass and know how to use them. Although this book doesn't cover everything you'll want to know about map-and-compass navigation, it will give you enough information to get by in a pinch.

If you want to know how to use GPS for recreational adventures such as hiking, backpacking, hunting, fishing, river rafting, kayaking, mountain biking, snowshoeing, outdoor photography, or the fast-growing sport of geocaching, this book is for you. The focus is on practical applications, not technical theory. You'll learn how to be successful and safe, and how to get the most enjoyment out of your investment. The theory covered in these pages is limited to what you need to know to achieve success. If you really want to delve into the gory technical details of such things as satellite PRN sequences or dilution-of-precision errors, there are plenty of advanced textbooks and websites to keep you occupied for months.

You don't even need to own a GPS receiver to get something out of this book. In fact, if you're thinking of making the investment but haven't yet done so, this book can help you make the best choice. Even if your partner is more interested in GPS than you are, you might want to pick up a copy. My wife never showed much interest in GPS until one day when she discovered the sport of geocaching. Now she's as likely to pull me along on an outdoor treasure hunt as I am to lead her into the backcountry. Geocaching is a great sport for the whole family, combining elements of a treasure hunt, outdoor exercise, and navigation skills in a form that helps you quickly gain GPS experience.

This book is organized into four parts, starting with the basics and building from there. Part I gives you the background behind what GPS is and how it is used. You'll learn what to look for in a GPS receiver and how to do basic things like marking and going to waypoints and following compass bearings.

Part II introduces the concepts of latitude and longitude, and how to use them to find a place you've never been to before. You'll learn the UTM system, an alternative to latitude and longitude developed by the military that has advantages for hikers and backpackers. This is also where you will learn about topographic maps and how to read waypoint coordinates from both paper and software maps.

Part III describes the critical wilderness navigation skills you should know if your GPS receiver fails in the backcountry. You will not only learn basic map-and-compass navigation, but also more primitive techniques and methods for avoiding disaster in the first place.

Part IV, which covers such topics as geocaching, GPS games, trail mapping, and highway navigation, shows you how to get the most out of your GPS receiver. You'll also discover the latest in equipment offerings from major manufacturers. Finally, two appendices and a glossary provide answers to frequently asked questions.

GPS has rightfully been called the greatest advance in navigation since the invention of the compass. Even if you never expect to use it for anything more complicated than getting back to your car in a crowded parking lot, you'll find it helpful. And once you know how to do that, it won't be long before you'll want to do more. Whatever your intended use, this book will help you get the most from your GPS receiver.

Stephen W. Hinch
Santa Rosa, California

Part 1
Basic Navigation

Key Concepts

▶ History of GPS

▶ How it works

▶ The four essential GPS skills

▶ Features of GPS receivers

▶ GPS limitations

▶ Waypoint basics

▶ Bearings: what they are and how to follow them

▶ MARK and GOTO: the two most important GPS functions

▶ All about compasses

▶ The difference between true and magnetic north

Basics of GPS

The Global Positioning System, a quick and easy way to find your position anywhere on earth, has revolutionized the art of finding your way in the outdoors. Whether you are a backpacker on a multiday trek or a mountain biker out for an afternoon ride, GPS can help you reach your destination and return safely, thanks to a system of two dozen satellites funded and maintained by the US government that orbit silently overhead.

The idea of using satellites for navigation has been around since at least the late 1950s, when those few satellites in orbit were still the size of basketballs and neither the US nor the USSR had yet launched a man into space. Throughout the 1960s, the Army, Navy, and Air Force all worked on various competing and incompatible systems. Government bureaucracy being what it is, it wasn't until 1973 that the Department of Defense decided it might be smart to combine all these efforts into a

GPS satellite (Lockheed Martin Space Systems Co.)

single program. Much to the Navy's chagrin, the Air Force got the nod to lead the development and operation of the new system, dubbed the Navstar Global Positioning System. Nowadays we just call it GPS.

Work progressed rapidly once the efforts were unified. The first prototype satellite was launched in 1978 and second-generation production versions were launched starting in 1989. The system was declared fully operational in 1995, after the last of the 24 second-generation satellites was deployed. The satellites have operational lives of between three and 10 years, so new ones are regularly launched to replace older ones before they go out of service.

GPS first gained worldwide fame in 1991 during Operation Desert Storm, the conflict that also brought us night-vision goggles and the Hummer. The viewing public was quickly captured by television images of armored units being guided with pinpoint accuracy across a featureless Iraqi desert. GPS was so useful in Desert Storm that the military soon ran out of receivers for the troops and had to buy more than 10,000 consumer GPS units to make up the difference.

The fact that there were even consumer GPS receivers available was not always a given. The military had imagined all sorts of ways GPS could be used against us by our enemies, and they were dubious about letting the technology loose on the public. But the 1983 downing of Korean Air Flight 007 by the Soviet Union removed any doubt. This tragedy arose in part because the 747's flight crew made a navigation error, and the xenophobic Russians shot them down. GPS, if it had been available, could have prevented that fatal mistake. As a result, President Reagan issued a directive that GPS signals be made available free of charge to the entire world, and the commercial market has flourished ever since.

But the military was still wary. From the outset, they planned for two versions of the system: a high-accuracy version available only to the military, and a separate civilian version whose accuracy could be degraded without affecting military operations. In the early years, they degraded the accuracy of the civilian system through a process known as Selective Availability, or SA. This artificial degradation reduced the accuracy from an inherent 50-foot capability to something around 300 feet—the length of a football field.

For wilderness navigation, a 300-foot error isn't catastrophic. If you can get within a few hundred feet of your destination, you ought to be able to figure out the rest of the way on your own. But for aircraft and ships, it could mean disaster. Predictably, SA caused considerable public outcry, particularly from commercial users. The Coast Guard and others even deployed their own enhancement to the system, called Differential

GPS, which could completely eliminate the effects of SA to help ships safely navigate through harbors.

Finally, after numerous studies and substantial lobbying, President Clinton ordered that SA be permanently turned off beginning May 2, 2000. The improvement since that time has been remarkable. While the stated accuracy of civilian GPS is about 50 feet, most of the time you can find your position to within 20 feet or less. In the meantime, the military figured out how to locally degrade the accuracy of civilian GPS wherever in the world they're currently doing battle, without affecting it for the rest of us.

How GPS Works

GPS works by the process of triangulation. (Technically, it is actually called trilateration because it calculates your position using distances rather than angles, but the concept is similar, and the terms are often used interchangeably.) It's the same theme you've seen in countless World War II movies. The heroic French resistance fighter hides in a farmhouse, using his clandestine radio transmitter to send vital military secrets to the Allies. All the while, the Nazis are driving around in a big truck, listening in and trying to pinpoint his position. They invariably find him, but not until after he has broadcast the critical information.

In this scenario, the Nazis are using a technique called radio direction finding. With a radio receiver and an antenna that's very sensitive to the direction it's pointed, you can determine the direction a radio transmission is coming from. If you take readings from several different locations and plot them on a map, you'll find the transmitter at the location where all the lines intersect.

GPS is similar, with one significant difference. Instead of measuring the direction to each GPS satellite, your receiver determines its distance from each of them. It does this by measuring the time it takes to receive each of their signals. Knowing the travel time of the signals and the speed of light, it can determine the distance to each satellite. It then has to figure out precisely where each satellite is located in the sky. For this, it uses accurate information about satellite orbits stored in its internal memory. Once it knows the locations and distances of at least three satellites, your receiver has everything it needs to calculate your position. The math is a little complicated, but that's something for your GPS receiver to worry about.

This only works if your receiver knows exactly when each satellite sent its signal and exactly when it was received, so accurate time is an essential part of the system. All GPS satellites carry atomic clocks synchronized to three billionths of a second. Your handheld receiver,

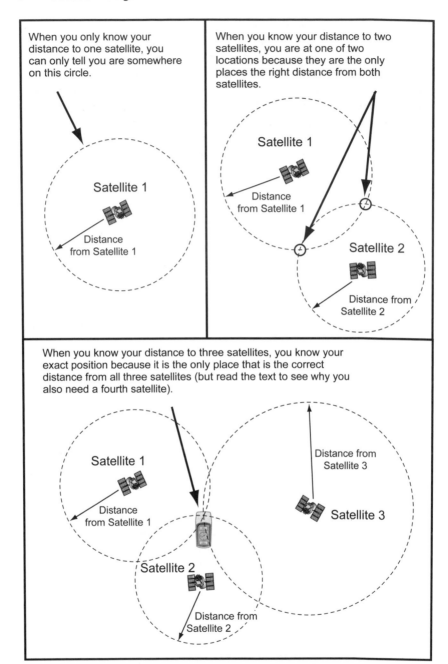

GPS works by a process of triangulation. To determine its position, a GPS receiver measures its distance from at least three satellites. There is only one location on earth that is the correct distance from all three satellites. A fourth satellite is necessary to correct timing errors in the system.

of course, doesn't include such a clock, but it doesn't need to. By tracking a fourth satellite, it can calculate its position multiple ways using all combinations of three satellites. This "redundancy" gives it enough information to eliminate the error in its internal clock. Without that extra satellite, your receiver won't be nearly as accurate; in some cases it could be in error by more than a mile. By the way, this ability to lock onto atomic clocks makes your GPS receiver the most accurate timepiece you can readily buy.

Parts of the System

There are three parts to the GPS system: the satellite segment, the user segment, and the control segment.

Satellite segment. Satellites are the heart of the Global Positioning System. They broadcast the signals your receiver uses to determine your position. (Chapter 2 looks at the different types of signals in more detail.) At least 24 satellites are in operation at all times, each orbiting the earth every 12 hours (or 11 hours and 58 minutes, if you really want to be precise). Their orbits are designed so that, theoretically, at least six and as many as 12 satellites arc above the horizon virtually all the time, regardless of where you are. "Theoretically" is the key word here—the satellite signals don't travel through mountains, buildings, people, or heavy tree cover, so unless you're on a flat plain or body of water, some signals probably will be blocked. Since your receiver must lock onto at least four satellites to accurately determine its position, you may have to move around to get better reception. (By the way, it's a little-known fact that all GPS satellites actually perform a second duty: Each includes an X-ray detector that lets the government monitor nuclear explosions anywhere in the world.)

User segment. Your handheld receiver makes up the user segment. There's a lot of power inside that little package. Not only does it contain a sensitive receiver capable of detecting signals less than a quadrillionth the power of a light bulb, it also includes a powerful computer that converts the raw data into such useful information as your position and speed. A GPS receiver doesn't include any kind of transmitter, meaning it is a passive positioning system—you can determine your own position but there's no way for anyone else to track you.

Control segment. This is what keeps the whole system running smoothly. Satellites need to be kept in their proper orbits and their signal transmissions kept up to date. The Air Force operates a series of five ground stations around the globe, typically at exotic tropical locations:

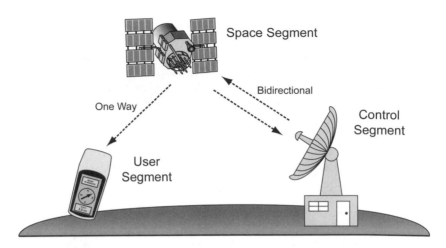

The three segments of the Global Positioning System

Hawaii, Ascension Island, Diego Garcia, Kwajalein, and the decidedly non-tropical master station in Colorado Springs. You'll probably never think about the control segment, but without it, the entire system would quickly fall into disrepair.

GPS Accuracy

It's surprisingly difficult to get a good answer on the level of accuracy of the Global Positioning System. Some sources say a consumer GPS receiver is accurate to within 100 feet. Others report it as 50 feet. Manufacturers often give even better numbers, in the vicinity of 20 feet or less. What's the true story?

First, don't depend on your receiver to tell you. Although many receivers report something called "Estimated Position Error" or EPE, it is not very accurate. This estimate is based only on satellite geometry and doesn't take into account the various other sources of error. Second, remember that until May 2, 2000, Selective Availability was the most significant source of error. Anything you read that was published before then is probably out of date.

The next thing to do is see what the Department of Defense says. After all, they operate the system, so they ought to know its performance, right? But they aren't as much help as you'd wish. In a typically conservative fashion, they don't actually specify total system accuracy, only the part within their direct control, which they call the Signal-in-Space, or SIS. This defines the accuracy of the signals as they radiate from the satellites, but it leaves out errors introduced as the signals propagate through the atmosphere.

Unfortunately, ever since the demise of Selective Availability, the atmosphere—especially the ionosphere—is the most significant source of GPS error. Just as the moon and sun look distorted as they drop low in the sky, signals from GPS satellites are bent as they travel through the atmosphere. They also experience delays that vary depending on the time of day, current solar activity, and moisture level in the air. Manufacturers of GPS receivers use mathematical models to predict and compensate for these errors, but atmospheric conditions are never truly constant.

The Defense Department estimates the accuracy of civilian GPS units to be better than 50 feet at least 95 percent of the time, anywhere in the world. This is what's called the 2drms (twice the distance root-mean-square) accuracy. It is based on statistics. Don't worry about the math. Just remember that the 2drms number means that over an entire day, a receiver's accuracy should be better than 50 feet at least 95 percent of the time.

Not all manufacturers specify their receivers this way. Some specify a simple rms value, which is half the 2drms number. This is a smaller number, but you will only see this accuracy two thirds of the time. Still others report a Circular Error Probable, or CEP. This is an even smaller number, but you will only be that close to your destination half the time. By specifying simple rms or CEP, manufacturers can make the numbers look better, but the receiver may not be any more accurate. The 2drms accuracy is a conservative number. It's twice as large as simple rms and 2.4 times larger than CEP accuracy for the same receiver.

Another unpredictable effect is called multi-path error. Satellite signals are reflected by such obstacles as tall buildings or canyon walls, and this can confuse your receiver as it tries to determine its distance from a satellite. Unfortunately, there's not much a receiver manufacturer can do to eliminate this error. You have to move your receiver away from the offending object.

If the government claims only 50-foot 2drms accuracy, you might wonder how manufacturers can claim better performance. Two factors come into play. First, the 50-foot number is a very conservative estimate that applies anywhere in the world. You would probably see such performance only on rare occasions. Second, manufacturers continue to improve their software models of the ionospheric effect, so today's receivers are slightly more accurate than those produced a few years ago.

While civilian receivers operate on a single frequency, called L1, at 1575.42 megahertz, military receivers use both L1 and a second frequency called L2, at 1227.6 megahertz. This second frequency contains an encrypted code available only to the military that allows the receiver to completely eliminate the effect of the ionosphere.

In spite of these accuracy ratings, consumer receivers will get you to within about 25 feet of your intended destination most of the time. While manufacturers will undoubtedly continue to improve their software, you won't see much more improvement without the help of DGPS or WAAS, two enhancements described in the next section. In 2005, the Defense Department began launching a new series of satellites giving civilians access to a second signal called L2C. When fully deployed in 2012, it will allow consumer receivers to eliminate ionospheric error, but you'll need a new GPS receiver to take advantage of this improvement. A third civilian signal called L5, at 1176.45 megahertz, will provide even higher accuracy for safety-of-life applications such as aircraft navigation.

There are a few things you can do to improve the accuracy of your measurements. First, try to make sure your receiver has a clear view of the sky and is tracking at least four satellites. More than four is even better—your receiver uses the extra satellites to further refine the accuracy of its measurements. Second, if your receiver has an "averaging" function, use it. (Usually, you'll find it labeled something like AVG as a selection on the MARK page.) The averaging function allows your receiver to accumulate many measurements over time and average them. Since GPS errors tend to be random, the longer you average, the more accurate will be your position. To be useful, you need to average for at least several minutes, and you must stay in one position during that period. Finally, although you can't depend on the EPE readout on your receiver to be a true representation of accuracy, it is a good relative indicator. Smaller numbers are better than larger numbers.

Finally, there is a difference between how accurately a receiver can determine its position and how accurately it will take you back to that position later. To understand why, refer to the diagram here. Suppose you want to record the coordinates of Position A, where you have just placed a hidden geocache. Because your receiver can only determine your position to within about 25 feet, the coordinates it gives you might be those of Position B, 25 feet away

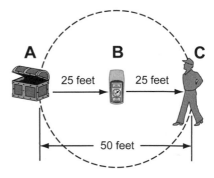

The error in returning to a previously marked waypoint is worse than the error in finding your absolute position, although you are unlikely to encounter this worst-case example.

from the true location. When you mark the position as Waypoint A, you are actually storing the coordinates of where your GPS receiver thinks it is—Position B—not where you actually are, Position A.

When you later want to find the geocache, you tell your receiver to go to Waypoint A. It will actually try to guide you to its stored location, Position B. But once again, because of system inaccuracies, you can only get to within perhaps 25 feet of that location. Depending on your luck, you could end up right on the treasure or as far away as Position C, which is 25 feet away from Position B and 50 feet away from your intended destination. In reality, you are unlikely to ever encounter this worst-case example. A more realistic estimate takes the receiver's specified accuracy and multiplies it by factor of 1.4. This suggests you should routinely be able to return to within 35 feet of a previously stored location. But just remember that once in awhile, your error will fall outside this estimate.

Improving GPS Accuracy: DGPS and WAAS

Today's basic 50-foot accuracy is sufficient for outdoor recreation, but it's still marginal for certain commercial uses, primarily involving air or sea navigation. Two enhancements have been made to improve system accuracy in certain situations. The first is the Coast Guard's Differential GPS, or DGPS. Although it was initially intended to guide ships on navigable waterways, it now extends to highway navigation as well. The Coast Guard operates more than 60 ground stations throughout the country, and the position of each has been accurately surveyed. Inside each station is a GPS receiver that compares the known location of the station with its position as measured by GPS. The difference is broadcast as a set of correction factors your receiver can use to improve its accuracy. DGPS allows you to reduce errors to just a few feet of uncertainty.

Unfortunately, to receive DGPS correction signals, you need a separate, specialized receiver connected to your main GPS receiver. (The additional DGPS receiver, together with its antenna, is so large you need a backpack to carry it, so it's not really a practical solution for wilderness navigators.) You also need to be within range of a ground station, so the technique has limited geographical coverage.

Another enhancement that's getting a lot of publicity these days is the Wide Area Augmentation System, or WAAS. It consists of 25 ground stations throughout the country as well as several satellites in high-altitude geostationary orbits over the equator. (Strictly speaking, WAAS refers to the system covering North America. The more general term is Satellite Based Augmentation System, or SBAS. You'll sometimes see it

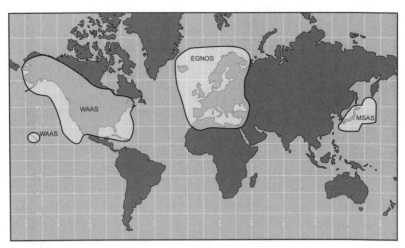

WAAS, EGNOS, and MSAS are all designed to improve the accuracy of civilian GPS.

called Wide Area DGPS, or WADGPS. The equivalent system in Europe is called EGNOS, while in Japan it is called MSAS.) Similar to DGPS, the ground stations measure the performance of the GPS system and determine correction factors to eliminate errors arising from current atmospheric conditions and system timing variations. Unlike DGPS, which broadcasts the correction factors from ground stations, WAAS corrections are sent to the geostationary satellites, which then broadcast them to your receiver. Again, accuracies of a few feet are achievable. Many newer GPS units can receive WAAS corrections without any additional equipment, making it more attractive than DGPS.

WAAS was primarily designed for aircraft navigation, although a lot of the publicity makes it sound like a panacea for all ills. Nonetheless, it's not all that useful for wilderness navigators. Only three satellites are visible from the US, and they're all low in the southern sky. This isn't a problem for aircraft, but in many areas of the country, the satellites aren't reliably visible from the ground. Another variant, Local Area Augmentation System, or LAAS, is even less useful. It's designed to guide aircraft on final approach and landing, so it operates only in the immediate vicinity of major airports.

Don't worry about using DGPS, WAAS, or LAAS in the outdoors. In fact, if you have a WAAS-enabled receiver, you may be better off disabling that feature and conserving battery power. I've never even needed WAAS accuracy to find hidden geocaches, which is probably the most exacting recreational use of GPS you're likely to do.

OTHER GPS-LIKE SYSTEMS

The fact that GPS is operated by the US Department of Defense causes concern in some countries. Two other GPS-like systems are currently being developed.

GLONASS is a Russian system that, like GPS, offers both civilian and military versions. When fully operational, GLONASS will consist of 24 satellites in three different orbital planes. As of 2007, only about half the satellites were operational, with full operation not scheduled until after 2009.

Another system, GALILEO, is being developed by the European Union. It will include a freely available coarse-positioning service and an encrypted, high-accuracy (to less than 1 meter) commercial service available for a fee. GALILEO is not expected to be fully operational until at least 2010. GPS, GLONASS, and GALILEO are all intended to be compatible, so that with the right receiver, you will be able to determine your position using any of the satellites visible from your current location.

GPS in the Wilderness: Essential Skills

In the simplest sense, a GPS receiver measures your exact position anywhere on earth, but navigation in the wilderness involves much more than knowing where you are. Now is a good time to introduce what I call the Cardinal Rule of GPS Navigation: *It doesn't do you any good to know where you are if you don't know where you want to go.*

The real contribution of GPS isn't showing you where you are, but showing how to get where you want to go. The problem is complicated by the fact that GPS receivers report numerous other pieces of information besides your current position. How do you know what's important and what isn't?

First remember that all GPS receivers really only measure three things: your position, your speed, and the current time. (More expensive receivers sometimes include a true magnetic compass and barometric altimeter, but these are completely separate instruments that don't use GPS to make their measurements.) All the other features—things like distance, bearing, map location, and even such vital details as sunrise and sunset or the best fishing times—are just calculations your receiver makes from those three measurements. That's why even the least expensive units work fine for outdoor navigators. They might not offer a lot of extras, but they all do the few things you really want.

So what are those few things? For outdoor navigation, there are only four things you should really know how to do with your GPS receiver. If you can do these, you can successfully navigate in the wilderness. They are:

▶ Know how to store your current location in GPS memory. This is known as marking a waypoint.

▶ Know how to get back to that stored location from wherever you might be. You'll do this by the technique of following a bearing.

▶ Know how to program into your GPS receiver the coordinates of locations you want to go to. This is known as entering a waypoint.

▶ Know how to navigate from one stored waypoint to the next in succession until you get to your final destination. This is known as following a route.

It's as simple as that. If you know how to do those four things, you'll be able to get where you want to go and return safely. Most of the rest of this book shows you how to do them. It also discusses the important topic of what to do when your GPS receiver fails. And to keep all this knowledge from going to waste, it ends up with some fun things to do with GPS.

THE FOUR ESSENTIAL GPS SKILLS

▶ Store your current location as a GPS waypoint
▶ Return to a stored waypoint by following a bearing
▶ Program waypoint latitudes and longitudes into your GPS receiver
▶ Navigate from one waypoint to the next in succession until you reach your final destination

GPS Receivers

You can buy a GPS receiver to fit almost any budget, from a basic, entry-level product for less than $100 to a deluxe model costing many hundreds of dollars. Not all of them are suitable for exploring the backcountry. In this chapter, you'll learn what you need to know about GPS receivers for the outdoors—what features are essential, which are merely nice, and what to avoid. First, though, you'll need to learn a bit more about how receivers work.

Satellite Signals

As you learned in Chapter 1, a GPS receiver works by measuring its distance from each of at least four satellites. Because it knows the exact location of each satellite, your receiver can calculate its position anywhere on earth. This is known as obtaining a position fix. But before this can happen, your receiver needs quite a bit of information from each satellite: its precise orbit, the time delay between when the satellite signal was sent

Tools of the outdoor navigator: map, compass, and GPS receiver

and when it was received, and the exact GPS time. Each satellite broadcasts several types of data. Once you see how this all works, you'll understand why your receiver sometimes gets a position fix right away and other times takes a lot longer.

Here's a brief description of the different types of data your receiver needs to calculate its position:

Almanac data. Although there are 24 satellites in the sky, their orbits are such that not all are simultaneously visible from any one location on earth. As few as six and at most 12 may be visible from your present location. It's hard enough for your receiver to detect signals that are actually there. To reduce the time wasted looking for satellites on the other side of the globe, your receiver stores a table of information about satellite orbits, called almanac data, which it uses to predict which satellites should be visible from your current position. It's not very precise information, but it's good enough to tell which satellites are above the horizon.

Your receiver gets its almanac data from the satellites themselves. Each satellite broadcasts the complete almanac for the entire array of 24 satellites, so you only need to be receiving one satellite to collect that information. Once your receiver has loaded a current almanac, the information stays valid for about six months. It's a good thing, too, because if you let the almanac get out of date by not using your receiver for an extended period, it takes at least 12.5 minutes to download a new one. If you ever find yourself in this situation, turn your receiver on, set it in a place where it has a clear view of the sky, and go have dinner. When you return, it should be finished downloading the new almanac. This is known as initialization.

You may also have to initialize your receiver if you've moved more than a few hundred miles from your last position. If you're in San Francisco and the last time you used it was in London, your receiver will still look for satellites that are above the horizon in London. After unsuccessfully searching for a few minutes, it may ask you to input the state or country you're in, and perhaps what time it is, before it can find its position.

Ephemeris data. Almanac data is not accurate enough for your receiver to determine your exact distance from a satellite. For this, your receiver needs very accurate satellite orbital information. Each satellite broadcasts information about its own orbit, called ephemeris data, which takes about 30 seconds to download. Your receiver needs ephemeris data from at least four satellites before it can find its position, so it can take as long as two minutes to acquire the necessary information.

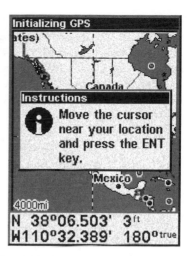

If you have moved more than a few hundred miles from your last position or have not used your receiver in several months, you may have to perform an initialization procedure. Mapping receivers like this Lowrance iFinder H20c make this easier by allowing you to move a pointer to your approximate position on the map screen.

Most receivers can speed the process by downloading from multiple satellites at once, reducing the total time to less than a minute. Ephemeris data stays valid for a few hours, so as long as you occasionally turn on your receiver during the day, you won't lose time waiting for this information to reload.

PRN code. This is the signal your receiver uses to measure the transmission time delay from each satellite. Civilian GPS units use a binary code that's 1023 bits long and takes 1 millisecond to transmit. (Military GPS uses a code that is six days long and much harder to jam.) PRN, which stands for "pseudo-random noise," is a noise-like signal that is relatively easy to detect and fairly difficult to jam.

Your receiver tracks these signals on up to 12 satellites simultaneously. But that's not all. The job is made even more difficult because all 24 satellites broadcast this information on exactly the same frequency. To understand the challenge this presents, think of it this way. Suppose you've just settled down in front of your TV to watch a rerun of your favorite TV show, *Friends*. But your TV isn't quite working properly, so when you turn it on, not only do you see *Friends*, you also get a ghost image of *Gilligan's Island* from the adjacent channel. Your job is to follow what's going on with Rachel and Ross while ignoring what's going on between the Professor and Mary Ann.

Your GPS receiver has a similar task, but the analogy is that instead of ignoring *Gilligan's Island*, it is enjoying both shows simultaneously. In fact, it's not really happy unless it's watching at least four shows, and it can watch up to 12 shows at once without losing track of what any of the characters in any of the shows is doing. It's the goal every good couch potato strives for—watching a dozen shows at once without ever having to use the remote control to switch between them!

Acquisition Time

The length of time it takes your receiver to find its position depends on how long it's been since you last used it. You'll often see manufacturers specify various acquisition times using terms like "cold start," "warm start," and "hot start." Although not always defined exactly the same way by every manufacturer, the following are typical definitions:

Cold start. Your receiver must perform a cold start when it has valid almanac data but no valid ephemeris data. In this case, it takes between 45 seconds and two minutes to find its position. Your receiver must perform a cold start if it hasn't been used in more than six hours but less than six months, when its almanac data expires.

Warm start. In this case, your receiver has valid almanac data, but the ephemeris data is valid only for three satellites. It has to download new ephemeris data from the fourth satellite, so it takes 15 to 30 seconds to find its position. Your receiver will typically perform a warm start if it has been between three and six hours since you last used it.

Hot start. When you turn your receiver on within a few hours from when it was last used, the almanac and ephemeris data stored in its memory are still valid. In this case, your receiver doesn't have to wait to download new ephemeris data and can find its position in only a few seconds. Ephemeris data remains valid for about three hours, so if it has been less than three hours since you last found your position, your receiver will perform a hot start.

When your receiver is downloading ephemeris data, it must receive a complete message from each satellite without interruption. Published acquisition times assume you are standing still with a clear view of the sky. When you are moving, acquisition may take considerably longer. If you momentarily lose the signal as you travel under a bridge or through tree cover, your receiver has to start over again. Depending on how often the signals are interrupted, acquisition can take many minutes. Also note that in all cases, the almanac data is assumed to be valid. As indicated earlier, without a valid almanac, it may take more than 12 minutes and as long as an hour to determine your position.

GETTING TO KNOW YOUR GPS RECEIVER

If you've just bought a new GPS receiver, now is a good time to get acquainted with it. Take it out of the box and scan the owner's manual to learn how to do things like load the batteries and turn it on. With some receivers, you have to accept a warning message by pushing the ENTER key before it will find your position. Others begin to acquire satellites immediately after being turned on. Don't be afraid to experiment and push buttons; you can't hurt your receiver by doing so, and you'll quickly become familiar with it.

The first time you take your receiver out of the box, you will probably have to initialize it. In the past, this was tedious. The receiver would display a map of the world, and you would have to move a cursor to your approximate location. It could then take many minutes to find your position. Most modern receivers perform an automatic initialization. All you do is go outside to give your receiver a clear view of the sky, turn it on, and wait a few minutes for it to acquire the satellites. When done, it will report that it has found your position and display your current latitude and longitude.

The next thing to do is learn how to scroll through the various screens, or "pages," of the display. Every GPS receiver works similarly: You push a button typically labeled something like PAGE or NAV to cycle through a series of pages that display information or allow you to perform various tasks. Each time you push the PAGE button, you move to the next page, eventually returning back to the first page. You can usually also cycle through the pages in reverse by pushing a button called QUIT or ESC.

Satellite Page   Trip Computer Page   Map Page

Main Menu Page   Altimeter Page   Compass Page

Continued on next page

A simple, non-mapping receiver has only a few pages. Mapping receivers add several additional pages. Every receiver typically includes at least the following pages:

SATELLITE page: This page shows you all the satellites your receiver is tracking and where they are located in the sky. Some satellite pages also show additional information such as your current latitude and longitude.

COMPASS page: This page looks like a compass, but think of it as a heading indicator, not a true magnetic compass. (See page 24.) When you are moving, it orients itself to your direction of travel. When you have initiated a GOTO function, it displays an arrow pointing in the direction of your destination.

MAP page: On a mapping receiver, this is where you see the map detail. On a non-mapping receiver, it is a blank slate that shows your track and the locations of stored waypoints.

TRIP INFORMATION page: This page shows a variety of information about your trip. You can typically customize the page to show such things as your location, speed, distance traveled, distance to destination, elevation, etc.

SETUP or MAIN menu page (Garmin receivers): This is where you customize your receiver for such things as latitude-longitude or UTM coordinates, map datum, north reference, etc. On Magellan and Lowrance receivers, this is not a separate page, but is instead accessed from the menu button.

On each page, you can access additional information by pushing the MENU button. (On grayscale eTrex receivers, this is not a separate button but is instead a pull-down menu icon at the upper right corner of the screen.) This allows you to customize the appearance of the page or change the displayed data. After you've made the desired changes, push the QUIT or ESC button to return to the main page.

Once you become familiar with the basic operation of your receiver, you will probably want to use the MENU button to make a few changes to the default configuration. (Read your owner's manual to learn how to do this.) Recommended changes include:

Compass heading: Out of the box, many receivers are configured to display bearings as cardinal points of the compass (north, south, east, west). You will want to change that to the much more useful QUIT format. In addition, the compass page can often be configured to display additional data. If so, set it up to display BEARING and DISTANCE to your next destination.

Continued on next page

Position format: Most receivers come preset to display degrees-decimal minutes, which is a good default format, but you should check to make sure that's what is set. Hikers and backpackers may want to change it to UTM.

Map datum: Out of the box it is WGS 84. If you need NAD 27 or some other datum, change it now.

Satellite view: Some receivers, most notably the least expensive members of Garmin's eTrex series, come preprogrammed to display a very simple satellite page of limited usefulness. Change it to the more detailed display showing the locations of the satellites in the sky and the strengths of their signals.

You're now ready to explore the other features of your receiver. The two most important are the MARK and GOTO (sometimes called FIND) functions, described elsewhere in this chapter. If they are not obvious buttons on your receiver, take the time to learn how to access these features now. Other useful buttons include IN and OUT (used to zoom in and out on the map page), and an arrow keypad that allows you to scroll around to different locations on a screen. Some receivers replace the keypad with a multipurpose joystick.

It's likely that you will eventually have questions about your receiver's operation that aren't answered in the owner's manual. If so, check the manufacturer's website for FAQs and other information. If one exists, you may also want to join an online forum that covers your receiver. For Garmin receivers, check the Google group at groups.google.com/group/alt.satellite.gps.garmin/topics, and for Magellan, at groups.google.com/group/alt.satellite.gps.magellan/topics. DeLorme also hosts a forum for their PN 20 and other products at forum.delorme.com.

Features of GPS Receivers

Like everything electronic, GPS receiver technology is rapidly advancing. Size, weight, and power consumption drop every year. It's now possible to buy a GPS receiver built into your wristwatch, your mobile phone, or your handheld two-way radio. Who knows what you're likely to see in the next few years.

For wilderness navigation, you don't really need a lot of receiver horsepower; you'll be more concerned with keeping down size and weight. Of course, if you can afford it, you'll certainly want to consider a receiver with more features, but the minimum feature set you need includes the ability to do the following:

▶ Report your position in latitude and longitude

▶ Accept different map datums. In North America the absolute minimum includes the two formats known as WGS 84 and NAD 27.

▶ Determine your speed and direction of travel

▶ Store the locations of numerous points of interest, called waypoints

▶ Calculate the direction and distance from your current location to any stored waypoint and from one waypoint to another

The Garmin Rino is a GPS receiver built into a two-way radio.

▶ Plot a "breadcrumb" trail, or track log, of your path as you move around

The next chapter covers waypoints and bearings; latitude and longitude, UTM, and map datums are covered in Chapter 4; and track logs are described in Chapter 12.

Today, GPS receivers for outdoor use come in two levels of complexity. Entry-level receivers are inexpensive units that provide all the basic features you need but not much more. Mapping receivers have the ability to display full-featured maps, including towns, rivers, roads, and sometimes topographic features. They typically come factory-loaded with a fairly simple base map of major North American cities and highways. By purchasing additional software, you can load more detailed street

When loaded with the appropriate software, mapping receivers can display detailed topographic maps. The DeLorme PN-20 can display scanned images from USGS 7.5-minute topo maps.

or topographic maps (limited only by the receiver's available memory). With the right map, a high-end mapping receiver can even give you turn-by-turn driving directions to any street address you enter, although it will only display text messages, not audible voice commands like those found in a dedicated highway navigation receiver. More expensive receivers may include additional features such as a barometric altimeter and a magnetic compass.

If you're looking to buy a used receiver, you may come across a third type, the so-called intermediate receivers. These include a simple database of towns and other points of interest, but they can't display detailed maps of roads or highways. A few intermediate receivers are still sold new, but as true mapping receivers have become more affordable, intermediate receivers have fallen from favor.

Outdoor navigation doesn't require a high-end receiver. As a minimum, you want one that is small and lightweight, has waterproof construction, and includes the minimum features listed on page 22. If you're only going to use it for outdoor recreation and can't afford to spend a lot of money, a basic, entry-level receiver will do fine. Ignore Internet reviews that disparage low-end products. Modern name-brand receivers work just fine, although there's always a chance you'll outgrow them and eventually long for more features. Extra gadgets like true barometric altimeters or magnetic compasses are fun toys if you can afford them, but hardly essential. That doesn't mean a magnetic compass isn't important—it is. It's just not necessary to have it built into your receiver. In fact, as I'll stress more than once, even if your receiver includes a built-in magnetic compass, my strong advice is that you still carry a separate compass. It's never smart to pin all your navigation hopes on the vagaries of a single, battery-powered electronic instrument, no matter how much you paid for it.

If you also intend to use your receiver for highway navigation, you'll want a more expensive unit with mapping capability. Here you'll have to make a trade-off. Smaller, lighter units have smaller screens that are a little harder to see while driving. (Be sure your passenger is the one looking at the screen while you're driving!) Larger units with bigger screens are great on the highway but cumbersome on a hike. In my opinion, smaller is better, so I'll take what I get while driving. But you may make a different compromise. Just make sure you don't buy a unit dedicated only for highway use that doesn't have the waypoint and tracking features you'll need in the wilderness. The following discussion shows you what to look for, starting with key GPS features. For detailed information on current models suitable for outdoor navigation, refer to Chapter 15.

Display

Less expensive receivers use black-and-white LCD displays. High-end receivers use color LCD displays that are optimized for viewing in bright sunlight. Color is an advantage in a mapping receiver that must portray a lot of information at once. In the past, color displays were difficult to read in bright sunlight, so if you're in the market for a used receiver, do your own tests before making a purchase.

Most receivers allow you to activate a backlight so you can read the display in dim light. Inexpensive receivers don't need to show a lot of data and can get away with low-resolution displays. Mapping receivers need higher resolution.

Antenna

Your receiver will use one of two types of antennas, either a quadrifilar helix antenna or a patch antenna. Quadrifilar helix antennas are coils of wire beneath a plastic cover that typically extend beyond the main body of the receiver. Sometimes they are detachable, which can be useful in an automobile. In other units, they are solidly attached but stick out from the top of the receiver.

Patch antennas look like small, rectangular metal sandwiches. They're easy to build into the main receiver unit, so if yours doesn't have some sort of appendage sticking out of it, it probably uses a patch antenna. Either kind works well if you hold the unit properly. Units with a patch antenna, like the

Compare the screen resolution of two Garmin receivers. The basic eTrex (left) is a non-mapping receiver with a low-resolution display. The GPSmap 60CSx is a mapping receiver that needs a high-resolution display. Despite their appearances, these compass displays do not completely eliminate the need for a separate magnetic compass.

The Garmin GPSmap 60CSx can be used with a separate external antenna. Note how the antenna cable has been routed under the D-ring on the back of the receiver to better protect the miniature MCX connector.

Garmin eTrex series, get best reception when held horizontally. Units with a quadrifilar helix antenna, like the Magellan Meridian series, typically should be held vertically. But this isn't always the case, so check your instruction manual for more information.

Some receivers have a connector that allows you to attach an external antenna. While not essential, this can be a useful feature. In a car, it allows you to place the antenna where it has a good view of the sky while keeping the receiver on a dashboard bracket for easy viewing. In the field, you can attach the antenna to your clothing and put the receiver in your pocket. This is great if you want to record a continuous track of your journey, such as when you're mapping out the complete route of a new hiking or biking trail. Any receiver placed in your pocket will likely lose satellite reception, so if you don't use an external antenna, you'll need to keep it out where it has a good view of the sky.

The satellite page shows the strength of each signal and the location of each satellite in the sky. This is the display on the DeLorme GPS PN-20.

Receiver

Inside the unit behind the antenna is the receiver system. All modern units have at least 12 channels so they can simultaneously track up to 12 satellites; some can even track 14 or 16 satellites, allowing them to get a position fix even faster. Some older models had only one- or two-channel receivers. But they still needed to track four satellites to get a position fix, so they had to sequentially switch between the different satellites. It's the equivalent of a TV couch potato trying to watch four different shows by using his remote control to switch through them in quick succession. Like the couch potato, these older receivers missed some information, so they took a lot longer to get a position fix and were never quite as accurate as true 12-channel receivers. If you're thinking of buying a used receiver, make sure it has 12 *parallel* channels. Be careful, because some receivers were advertised as being able to "track up to 12 satellites" but could only track two satellites at a time.

Receiver technology, like all electronics, constantly improves. Some of the newest receivers have much improved sensitivity and can lock onto satellites even indoors or under heavy tree cover. If this is important to you, look for a product that uses a high-sensitivity GPS receiver chip such as the SiRFstarIII from SiRF Technology or the Hammerhead from Global Locate.

Memory

A mapping receiver's built-in map (known as a base map) doesn't contain a lot of detail. It is typically limited to interstate highways, a few arterial roads, and major cities. If you want to do serious road navigation or view topographic contours, you need to load more detailed maps into its memory. Not just any map will do; you must buy the software from your receiver's manufacturer. Using a computer, you can then load more detailed maps. The amount of detail is limited by your receiver's memory. With 8 megabytes you might be limited to the streets of a single city. With 64 megabytes you could load a significant part of a state. Even with a 64-megabyte receiver, on a long cross-country trip you might need to bring along a laptop computer to occasionally load new maps.

Some mapping receivers such as this Lowrance iFinder H20c can accept external memory cards. (Courtesy of Lowrance)

The trend these days is for receivers to accept external memory cards. This is very convenient because you can easily swap maps without the need for a computer. Garmin receivers typically use MicroSD cards, while Lowrance, Brunton, and Magellan use standard SD cards. Before leaving on your trip, store as many maps as necessary onto memory cards (you may need several cards, depending on the extent of your journey). Then when you need a new map, just swap cards.

Mapping receivers from most major manufacturers only accept maps from their own proprietary software programs. (Magellan's Triton series is an exception; they work specifically with National Geographic maps.) Each company offers various types of maps covering such things as metropolitan streets, highway points of interest, topographic features, or marine navigation aids and obstructions. Unfortunately, if you also use one of the excellent third-party topographic mapping software programs such as National Geographic's Topo! or Maptech's Terrain Navigator, you'll be disappointed to learn that while they'll let you upload waypoints and routes into your receiver, you won't be able to upload the maps themselves.

Computer Port

Many receivers let you transfer data between your receiver and your personal computer. You can send information both ways—download stored waypoints, tracks, and routes from your receiver to your PC, and upload them from your PC to your receiver. You'll need two things to do this: some sort of software program to handle the exchange, and a data cable to connect your receiver to the PC. Most software programs have been designed for Windows PCs. Mac support is much harder to find.

You can get the software either from the receiver manufacturer or from third parties like National Geographic (maps.nationalgeographic. com/topo) or DeLorme (www.delorme.com). Remember that if you want to load actual maps into a mapping receiver (as opposed to just transferring waypoints, routes, and track logs), you're stuck with mapping software from the receiver manufacturer.

Modern GPS receivers connect to a computer through the USB interface. This is a fast, efficient way to transfer data. You'll still find some receivers that use the old RS-232 serial port. There are a couple of problems with this approach. First, the transfer rate is excruciatingly slow. This is tolerable if you're only transferring waypoints and track logs, but transferring 24 megabytes of map data takes over an hour. Second, serial ports are old technology, and most new PCs don't even come with one. It is possible to use a USB-to-serial converter, but manufacturers caution that not all such converters will work with their receivers. And even if it does work, you won't get the transfer speed of true USB; it is still limited to that of the serial port. If you're going to transfer much data between a GPS receiver and a computer, look for a receiver with a USB interface.

Power

As receivers continue to get smaller and lighter, their power requirements are also dropping. It wasn't long ago that the smallest receivers were powered by four AA cells. Now they use only two AA cells, and some even use AAA cells. A minor trade-off is that battery life is sometimes shorter, although improvements in receiver technology continue to reduce power requirements. With a newer receiver you can expect to get a minimum of 15 to 20 hours out of a set of alkaline batteries, and a bit less with rechargeable NiMH batteries. If you're wondering how you'll get through a three-day hike with a receiver that only runs for 15 hours, understand that you shouldn't need to leave it on all the time. Just turn it on for a few minutes whenever you need a position fix or an updated bearing and distance to your destination. With this approach, you should be able to get through even a two-week journey without problems. If you're concerned, you can always pack extra batteries.

It's a little different if you're using your receiver in a car. In this case, you'll probably leave it turned on for extended periods, so you'll want to spend extra money on a cable that lets you plug it into your car's cigarette lighter. If this kind of use is important, make sure to buy a receiver that can operate from an external power source.

Water Resistance

Buy a receiver designed to be waterproof. Even if you don't intend to take it on a lake or river, you don't want it to be damaged by rainfall or an accidental coffee spill. The relevant industry standard is known as IEC 60529 IPX7. Receivers meeting this standard can survive accidental immersion in 1 meter of water for up to 30 minutes. They are not intended for continuous underwater use, but since GPS signals don't travel underwater, this level of protection isn't necessary. Note that the IEC standard doesn't require that the unit float. Some do, some don't, so if you plan to use it in a kayak or boat, you might want to make sure your chosen unit is designed to float, not plummet to the bottom, if accidentally dropped overboard.

Data Reporting and Analysis

Most GPS receivers designed for outdoor use can give you far more information than you're ever likely to need. The following list is useful in helping you weed out receivers that really aren't intended for wilderness navigation. All of these features will be discussed more fully in later chapters. Here's what to look for:

Position format in latitude and longitude. Most people will never need to use anything else, although inveterate backpackers occasionally swear by the UTM coordinate system. Any good unit will also have a dozen or more other formats that look good on the data sheet but will probably never get used—the West Malayan RTO and the EOV Hungarian Grid are two that come to mind.

A typical GPS receiver can display a wide variety of data about your trip. The TRIP COMPUTER screen of the Garmin eTrex Vista allows you to customize the displayed data. Most of this information will only be accurate if you remember to clear memory before starting on your trip.

Map datum choices that include at least WGS 84 and NAD 27. WGS 84 is the native datum of the GPS system, and NAD 27 is a North American datum used on many older topographic maps. Travelers to the United Kingdom who use local maps will need the datum called "Ordinance Survey GB," while travelers elsewhere in Europe may need the "European Datum 1950." In Japan, the "Tokyo Datum" may be useful. Datums are covered in more detail in Chapter 4. As with position format, most receivers provide dozens of other datums, including such all-time favorites as Liberia 1960 and Ascension Island 1958. Admittedly, a few of these will be important if you intend to do much international travel, but mostly they just clutter up the screen and make it harder to find those you really need.

Ability to mark and store waypoints. This is one of the two most important features you'll use. You'll learn more about waypoints in the next chapter. Look for a receiver that can store at least 500 waypoints.

Map Datum
WGS 84 - Default
North American 1927 - Me
North American 1983 - Ala
Adindan - Mean for Ethiop
Adindan - Burkina Faso
Adindan - Cameroon
Adindan - Ethiopia
Adindan - Mali
Adindan - Senegal
Adindan - Sudan
Afgooye - Somalia
Ain el Abd 1970 - Bahrain
Ain el Abd 1970 - Saudi A
Anna 1 Astro 1965 - Coco
Antigua Island Astro 1943
Arc 1950 - Mean for Botsı

GPS receivers like this Lowrance iFinder H2Oc typically offer 100 or more datum choices.

Easily accessible GOTO (sometimes called FIND) function. This is the second of the two most important GPS features, as it allows you to find the distance and bearing to your destination. Chapter 3 covers how to use this function. Once upon a time, all self-respecting receivers had dedicated GOTO buttons, but nowadays some of the smaller ones have given this up—you'll have to search for it buried among the various screen displays. High-end receivers often label this a FIND button. With this function, the receiver can tell you not only how to get to waypoints, but also, with the right map loaded in memory, how to get to addresses and points of interest.

North reference. At minimum, you should be able to select between true north and magnetic north, as discussed in the next chapter.

Compass display. This is where you'll find the two most important pieces of data you'll normally need: the bearing and distance to your intended destination. Although it's not a substitute for a true magnetic compass, which tells you the direction it's pointing, the compass pointer is still useful. When you're moving, it does a pretty good job of showing you the direction to your destination. When you're stopped, though, it's useless. The compass display tells you only the direction you're moving, not the direction the receiver is pointing. For applications such as geocaching, when you're not likely to get lost, you may be able to get by with this display in place of a magnetic compass. For any serious wilderness navigation, though, you should carry a separate compass. Many receivers allow you to change this display from one that looks like a compass to one that looks like a highway. Stick with the compass display.

Route capability. This is a useful tool to guide you on a multipart hike. It's like an enhanced GOTO function. You specify the waypoints you want to go to and the sequence in which you want to reach them; the route function automates the process of going to each of them in succession. You could, of course, do the same thing manually, but you're less likely to make a mistake if you've entered the information as a route.

Any receiver that offers all of these features will probably offer many others. Some are useful, but most are just niceties. Sunrise, sunset, time of day, and trip odometer, for example, could provide useful information. Glide ratio, velocity made good, and estimated time of arrival are really designed for aircraft or marine navigation and won't have much use in the outdoors.

WAAS reception. As described in Chapter 1, WAAS is operated by the Federal Aviation Administration to improve GPS accuracy for aircraft navigation. Using WAAS, it is possible to improve measurement accuracy to better than 3 meters (10 feet).

It sounds great, but because the geosynchronous satellites orbit over the equator, they appear low in the sky to ground-based observers in the US. They are often blocked by the surrounding terrain, trees, or buildings, making WAAS marginally useful for outdoor enthusiasts. It was developed for aircraft navigation, and that is where it really shines.

Although most GPS receivers for the outdoor market include WAAS capability, it is hardly essential. In fact, it is even possible that WAAS signals could reduce your accuracy if you are outside the US. Since all the WAAS ground stations are located in North America, the WAAS correction factors are only valid within this region. But they can still be received even when you are in Mexico or South America. If you have WAAS turned on, your receiver will apply these invalid correction factors, which could actually make your accuracy worse. For these reasons, it is often better to turn WAAS off so you can get faster position fixes and consume less battery power.

Limitations of GPS

GPS is so powerful, it's easy to forget it also has limitations. These are especially likely to show up in wilderness navigation, so it's important you understand and know how to deal with them.

Satellite visibility. Since it depends on satellites to operate, your receiver needs a clear view of the sky. It doesn't need to see the whole sky, but at least enough to lock onto four different satellites. So if you're in a narrow canyon or surrounded by tall buildings, your receiver probably won't work. Nor will it work indoors. And it might not work under heavy tree cover because the water in tree leaves blocks the satellite signals. In a leafy forest, your receiver will work better in the fall and winter, when the leaves have fallen from the trees. On the other hand, clouds, rain, and snow won't significantly affect your reception. A solid film of water blocks the signals, but water vapor or isolated droplets don't. That's also why you can't use a GPS receiver under water.

This is one area where a larger receiver might work better because it will probably have a more sensitive antenna. Some newer receivers use very sensitive, integrated circuits from SiRF Technology or Global Locate that work much better indoors and under heavy tree cover. But even the best receiver won't work in all cases. The satellite page on your receiver will help you see how good your reception is. Check it occasionally. With practice, you'll get good at predicting when you're about to lose coverage.

Requires at least four satellites. For best accuracy, your receiver must be locked onto at least four satellites. This is called the "3D operating mode" because it accurately finds your position in all three dimensions. But sometimes terrain or tree cover will block some signals, and your receiver won't lock onto four satellites. If it can lock onto three satellites, it will operate in what's known as "2D mode." It will still calculate a position, but it probably won't be very accurate. In 2D mode, your receiver compensates for the

Be sure you know how to tell if your receiver is operating in 3D mode. The Lowrance iFinder (top) explicitly indicates its state. On the Garmin eTrex Vista (bottom), you must observe the satellite strength indicators to confirm that at least four satellites are being tracked.

missing satellite by estimating your elevation. However, the only elevation it knows is the last one it measured, so that's what it uses. But if you've changed your position since then, your elevation could have changed by hundreds or thousands of feet, and the calculated position can be off by a mile or more. If you know your current elevation, you can somewhat improve accuracy by manually entering it into your receiver. But in general, 2D navigation is nearly useless and even dangerous for wilderness navigation, so never depend on it.

If 2D mode is so useless, why do manufacturers provide it? It does work on the ocean, where the elevation is constant. But ironically, it's almost never necessary on the ocean, since you almost always have a clear view all the way to the horizon, making it easy to lock onto four satellites. 2D mode is a holdover from the early days of GPS, before all 24 satellites were deployed. There's little need for it today.

Manufacturers don't do a very good job of explaining this limitation. Instruction manuals often refer to the fact that "elevation is not being computed," but they don't explain the impact on accuracy. Some newer units don't even explicitly tell you whether they're operating in 2D or 3D mode. You have to figure it out for yourself by looking at the satellite page to see how many satellites are being tracked. Make sure you know how to confirm your receiver is operating in 3D mode before you rely on its data.

Inaccurate elevation. GPS was designed to find your position anywhere on earth, but it was not designed to accurately measure your elevation. All GPS receivers will give you an elevation readout, but you can't depend on it. Its accuracy depends on the geometry of the satellites in the sky. When they are well spread out, it can be reasonably accurate, but when they are closely grouped, it can be off by a thousand feet or more. If you really want accurate elevations, you'll need to use a calibrated barometric altimeter (some more expensive units come with one built in).

It's not a compass. Remember that a GPS receiver is not a compass. This is confusing to many people because every receiver has a screen that looks like a compass display. But this screen only tells you what direction you're moving, not what direction the unit is pointed. So it is really a heading indicator, not a true compass. To navigate safely in the wilderness, even with a GPS unit, you must be able to accurately determine direction, so you should always carry a separate magnetic compass.

Today, some receivers include a built-in magnetic compass. Known as an electronic fluxgate compass, it is accurate to within about 5 degrees. But when turned on, it rapidly uses up batteries. While a receiver with a built-in magnetic compass can cost over $50 more than a similar one without it, you can buy a quality magnetic compass for under $20. If you have a unit with a built-in compass, go ahead and use it, but still carry a separate compass. That way, if your receiver gets damaged or its batteries fail, you're not completely helpless.

Navigation Using Waypoints and Bearings

The simplest thing you can do with your GPS receiver is find your way back to a place you've been to before—a favorite campsite, fishing spot, or even your car in the mall parking lot. I call this "basic navigation" because you can use it without knowing anything about such things as latitude, longitude, position formats, UTM, or map datums. You just need to know how to store your current location as a GPS waypoint and how to return to it using your receiver's GOTO function. You'll also need to know how to navigate by following a bearing. So this chapter covers waypoints, bearings, and your receiver's MARK and GOTO functions.

Consider an example: Suppose you intend to spend the afternoon exploring unfamiliar territory. Maybe you're a hunter going where the game takes you or a photographer looking for that great shot. Either way, you don't have a planned itinerary and might not follow established trails. You need to make sure you can get back to the trailhead before dark. So here's what to do: Store the location of the trailhead as a GPS waypoint before you start out. When you're ready to return, let your receiver show you how to get back to it. If you know how to follow a bearing, you should have little trouble getting back.

Waypoints

Waypoints (sometimes called landmarks or points of interest) are one of the most basic GPS concepts. Think of it as something like a street address. Suppose you live at 123 Center Street, Anytown, USA. Your address is simply a way to describe exactly where you live. It's how the post office knows where to deliver your mail, how the pizza parlor knows where to deliver that delicious dinner you ordered.

Waypoints are the GPS equivalents of street addresses, but of course they aren't just limited to streets. The Global Positioning System uses a mathematical model of the entire earth to describe the coordinates of any point on it. Most often, this will be in the form of latitude and longitude, but your GPS receiver can use many other formats as well. In fact, regardless of what format you specify, your receiver always stores the information in its own internal format referenced to the center of the earth. It applies complicated mathematical formulas to convert this internal format into something more useful to humans, like latitude and longitude or UTM coordinates.

Using waypoints, it's possible to do things like record the position of a tree in your front yard separately from another tree in your backyard. But remember, GPS accuracy is only about 25 feet, so don't depend on it to determine positions better than that. You can't use your consumer GPS receiver to accurately survey your property lines, for example, although it is possible to do so with certain very expensive commercial units and additional computer software.

A typical consumer GPS receiver can store 500 or more locations in its waypoint database. You can store them in several ways. The simplest way, though not always the easiest, is to go to the desired location and push the buttons that tell your receiver to store your current location in memory. That's what is covered in this chapter. Chapter 4 will show you how to enter the latitude and longitude or UTM coordinates of a location without actually having to go there. Chapter 7 will teach you how to use a computer and mapping software to upload waypoints without having to arduously key in the numbers.

Once you've stored a waypoint, you can go wherever you want, and your GPS receiver can always show you how far away and what direction that waypoint is from your current position. Then it's a simple matter of heading in the right direction until you get back to it. But to do this, you need to know a bit about direction-finding in the wilderness.

Directions and Bearings

We are all familiar with how to describe directions in terms of the four cardinal points of the compass—north, south, east, and west. Intermediate directions include northeast, southeast, southwest, and northwest. Many GPS receivers even let you display bearings in this format. But it's not very precise.

Compass rose

You can use a map to read the bearing from your current position to your destination. Draw a straight line between the two points and center a protractor over your current position with 0° oriented due north. Read the bearing where the line intersects the edge of the protractor.

A better way is based on the Greek system of dividing the full circle into 360 degrees. North is defined as the reference direction at 0°. Going clockwise around the circle, east is at 90°, south at 180°, and west at 270°.

With this approach, you can describe a direction very accurately. A mountain in the distance that's directly east of you is said to be at a bearing of 90°. Another peak that's directly southwest is at a bearing of 225°. With care, using a good magnetic compass, you can measure the bearing to a distant object to an accuracy of about 2 degrees. You'll learn how to do that later in this chapter.

In GPS terminology, the term "bearing" is used to describe the direction between your current position and your desired destination. In contrast, the term "heading" describes the direction you are actually traveling. (Purists use the term "azimuth" instead of bearing, and "track" instead of heading, but the terms "bearing" and "heading" have become dominant in the GPS world.) If you're moving directly toward your destination, then your heading and your bearing are the same. If not, they will be different. Often, you can't head directly along your desired bearing, as when you're navigating around an obstacle such as a mountain.

You can set up your GPS receiver to display either value on its screen (see the figure on page 24). Just make sure you understand the difference between the two terms, and that you use bearing, not heading, to guide you to your destination.

When set to display numeric bearings, your GPS receiver can give you a bearing readout to 1-degree resolution. This is more than sufficient for outdoor navigation, where you'll rarely be able to follow a bearing to an accuracy of better than 5 degrees anyway.

Remember that the bearing to an object is a relative, not an absolute number—it depends on where you are. If you're in San Francisco, for example, the bearing to Denver is about due east, or 90°. But if you're in Washington, DC, Denver is about due west, or 270°. So the bearing between you and a target object changes as you move around. Someone standing in a different spot will measure a different bearing to the same object. If the two of you are close together and the object is far away, the difference won't be much, but it's always something to keep in mind.

Once you understand the concept of bearings, you can use a map and protractor to find the bearing from your present position to any destination. Here's how: Using a ruler, draw a straight line on the map connecting your current position with your destination. Now take a protractor (those circular plastic things with numbers on them that you haven't used since grade school) and center it over your current position. Orient it so that 0° points straight north. The bearing to your destination is where the line you drew intersects the edge of the protractor. Check the illustration on page 35 to see how this works. Once you understand it, you're ready to learn how to navigate.

Simple GPS Navigation

Waypoints and bearings are fundamental to the concept of GPS navigation. To see why, let's go back to our example. Recall that you plan to spend the afternoon exploring unfamiliar territory and want to make sure you can get back to the trailhead before dark. So you need to store the location of the trailhead as a GPS waypoint. When you're standing at the trailhead, this turns out to be pretty easy. You don't need to know anything about latitude or longitude. Just turn on your receiver, wait for it to find its position, then push the buttons to store that location in memory. This is known as marking a waypoint.

Every receiver does this a little differently. Some have a dedicated MARK button; push it and it brings up the waypoint screen. Here you can do things like give the waypoint a name or assign it a symbol before you store it. Other receivers don't have a dedicated button; you must select the MARK feature located on one of the menu pages. Such receivers usually have a shortcut way to mark a waypoint, such as by holding down the ENTER key for a couple of seconds. You'll need to read your instruction manual for specific details.

By default, your receiver will identify the waypoint by assigning it a number, but this really isn't very useful. After a day of hiking, how likely are you to remember you car is at waypoint number 743? So you

On the Garmin eTrex Venture Cx, you access the MARK WAYPOINT screen from the MAIN MENU. You can also reach it by holding down the thumb stick for two seconds.

should give it a better name. Older receivers often limit you to six alphanumeric characters, although newer units usually allow more. Again, check your manual to see how to enter waypoint names for your unit.

Regardless of which receiver you own, entering waypoint names is usually a cumbersome process involving lots of button-pushing. You'll need quite a bit of practice before you feel comfortable doing it. In Chapter 7, you'll see how to use a computer to make the job easier.

There are a couple of things to remember when storing waypoints. First, make sure your receiver is operating in 3D mode, not 2D mode. Many receivers have an explicit 2D-3D indicator, but some don't. In that case, you might need to check the satellite page to verify it is tracking at least four satellites. Or check the value your receiver reports for its Estimated Position Error (sometimes labeled "EPE" or "Accuracy"). If it's in the neighborhood of 20 to 30 feet or less, you're OK.

One more caution: Don't use the same name as a waypoint already stored in memory. Most receivers won't erase the existing waypoint, but they don't always make it obvious that they haven't stored the new one. This is most often a problem if you use the same name repeatedly, such as "CAR," to indicate the location of your car. Check the list of existing waypoints and delete any previous waypoint with the same name. Many Garmin receivers have a nifty feature called REPOSITION HERE. You just call up an existing waypoint and with one touch, you can move that waypoint to your current location.

Once you've stored the location of the trailhead, you are ready to go out and explore. Turn off your receiver and put it in your pocket. There's no reason to keep it turned on all the time unless you really want to record a complete track log of your journey as described in

Chapter 13. Leaving it on quickly uses up your batteries, and you probably won't get very good reception anyway if it's packed away in a pocket or backpack.

GOTO *Function*

After a few hours of exploration, you're ready to return to the trailhead. Now it's time to turn on your receiver and use another important GPS feature, the GOTO function. With this feature, you tell your receiver which waypoint you want to go to, and it automatically calculates the bearing and distance to it. Then you just follow the indicated bearing until you reach the car. (More on following bearings in a moment.)

Again, you need to read your instruction manual to learn how to use your receiver's GOTO function. Some receivers have a dedicated GOTO button: You just push the button and choose your desired waypoint. With other units,

The GOTO function is an essential feature. Know how to use it. The Magellan eXplorist 200 (left) has a dedicated GOTO button. On the Garmin eTrex (right), it is a selection on the WAYPOINT screen.

Mapping receivers such as this GPSmap 60CSx often replace the GOTO button with a FIND button, allowing you to find such things as cities, street addresses, and points of interest, in addition to waypoints.

you first have to select the desired waypoint from a waypoint database, either by spelling it or choosing from a list of nearby or recently visited waypoints. When it is displayed, one of the options you can select is GOTO.

On mapping receivers, the GOTO button is often replaced by a FIND button, which allows you to select from a variety of choices that can include waypoints, street addresses, cities, and other points of interest. After choosing WAYPOINTS and selecting the desired waypoint, you then choose GOTO. If your receiver can do turn-by-turn highway navigation, you will also have to make an additional decision of FOLLOW ROAD or OFF ROAD. Use OFF ROAD for outdoor navigation. It shows you the direct

NAVIGATION PRACTICE

If you have a GPS receiver, now is a good time to practice what you've just learned about using the MARK and GOTO functions.

1. Step outside your house so you have a clear view of the sky, then turn on your GPS receiver. Wait for it to lock on to the satellites and obtain a position fix. (If this is the first time you've turned it on, you might need to perform an initialization. You'll need to read your instruction manual to learn how to do this.) You should see a display showing the latitude and longitude of your current position (you may have to scroll through several pages to find it).

2. Store this location as a GPS waypoint. If your receiver has a MARK button, this is easy—push the button to call up the MARK WAYPOINT screen. If your receiver doesn't have a MARK button, it will probably have a menu page that offers several options, one of which is MARK. (You may have to read your receiver's instruction manual to learn where it is.)

   Once the MARK WAYPOINT screen is displayed, you are ready to save your position as a waypoint. But before doing so, change the name of the waypoint to "HOME" by highlighting the waypoint name and manually entering the word "HOME." Read the instruction manual if you are not sure how to do this. Once you have renamed it, save the waypoint by selecting the SAVE or OK option. You may want to check the waypoint database to make sure it has been saved.

3. Now take a short walk to the end of the block. After you've gotten a few hundred feet from your home, you are ready to find your way back by activating the GOTO function. If your receiver has a GOTO or FIND button, use it to select the waypoint called HOME. If not, call up your receiver's waypoint database and select the waypoint called HOME. (Again, if you're not sure how to do this, review the instruction manual.) One of the choices on the screen should now be GOTO. Select it, and you should be rewarded with a display showing the bearing and distance back to HOME.

bearing and distance to the selected waypoint. The FOLLOW ROAD choice is what to use when you are driving, which is covered in Chapter 14.

It's important to realize that when navigating in the outdoors, your receiver will only show you the straight-line direction and distance to your destination. It won't guide you along the path of a meandering trail or river. The section "Common Sense Navigation: Following a Bearing" on page 48 describes how to follow a GPS bearing over real terrain to reach your destination.

Once you've initiated the GOTO function, you should see the bearing and distance to the selected waypoint, although you might have to scroll through various pages to find the information. Usually, it will at least show up on the compass page, although with some receivers you have to make sure you have configured the display to show a bearing rather than some dubious piece of information like "glide ratio" or "estimated time en route." Once again, check your unit's instruction manual.

The compass page shows you the distance and bearing to a selected waypoint. This is the display from the DeLorme PN-20.

OK, that's great. You now know the bearing and distance to your destination. But how do you know which direction to hike? For that, you need to know how to use a compass to find and follow a bearing.

Using a Magnetic Compass

While you can often use your GPS receiver's compass page to follow a bearing in the field, you really should understand how to use a magnetic compass. As I've already said, for any serious navigation you absolutely must carry a separate compass. So let's take a few minutes to understand compasses and how to use them.

Compasses come in many flavors, from dime-store novelties to precision instruments costing many hundreds of dollars. Geologists and foresters swear by the Brunton Pocket Transit, a survey-grade compass that not only finds direction but also can be used to measure angles, height, and slope. It works great in the outdoors, but it's heavy, inconvenient, and pricey. You can get by with something much simpler and less expensive.

The Brunton is an example of a sighting compass, a class that also includes various military-type instruments. They are designed to read bearings to a precision of a degree or less, which can come in handy if you're trying to direct an air strike onto an enemy stronghold while avoiding friendly troops nearby. But it's overkill for wilderness navigators who usually aren't able to follow a bearing to better than 5 degrees anyway.

The best choice for recreational outdoor use is a type called the baseplate compass. (You'll sometimes hear it described as an orienteering compass.) Conveniently, you can get a good baseplate compass for less than $20, and even the top-of-the-line units rarely cost more than

$50. Popular manufacturers include Brunton, Silva, and Suunto.

If wilderness navigation only consisted of knowing which way was north, then just about any compass would do. But in reality, navigation involves two very important steps: First you must determine the bearing from your present location to your destination. Then you have to decide what direction that is in real life. The advantage of a baseplate compass is it can help you in each of these situations. It will also help on those occasions in the field when you want to read the bearing from your current position to an object like a mountain or radio tower in the distance.

Study a baseplate compass, and you'll see it has three parts: the baseplate, a compass vial, and a magnetic needle. The cylindrical compass vial contains the all-important magnetic compass needle. The vial is filled with liquid and has degree markings from 0 to 360 on its perimeter. The liquid damps the motion of the needle so it quickly stabilizes its position. (Compare this to cheap compasses in which the needle gyrates wildly at the slightest motion, and you'll appreciate the improvement.) The vial is designed so you can rotate it by hand, but with enough friction so that once positioned it stays put. Look through the vial to its bottom and you'll see what looks like the outline of a compass needle pointing to the 0° indicator on the perimeter of the vial. This is the north reference indicator. I'll explain how to use it in a minute.

The baseplate compass is the best choice for general outdoor use. On this Suunto GPS Plotter, the entire end of the baseplate is shaped like an arrow, making it easy to determine the direction of travel.

Components of a baseplate compass

Now let's look at the baseplate. The most important thing you'll see on it is a direction-of-travel arrow. On most compasses, the arrow is printed along the center of the baseplate, pointing away from the vial, but sometimes the end of the compass itself is shaped like an arrow. The opposite end of the arrow butts up against the compass vial at what is called a bearing indicator. This is what you use to find the direction to your destination. The baseplate also has at least one straight edge you can use to read bearings on a map.

Some compasses include a sighting mirror. This makes it easier to take accurate bearings in the field because when you tilt the mirror at about a 45-degree angle and hold the compass at eye level, you can look at both the compass vial and the object whose bearing you want. It's nice, but it's not an essential feature.

A sighting mirror makes it easier to take accurate bearings in the field. An added benefit is that when the cover is opened all the way, it becomes a long straightedge for measuring bearings on a map.

True vs. Magnetic North

Navigating with a compass would be easier if its magnetic needle always pointed to the North Pole, but it doesn't. For various complicated magnetohydrodynamic reasons, the earth's magnetic field isn't exactly aligned with its axis of rotation. This means a magnetic compass doesn't point to the true North Pole but rather to a location in northern Canada called magnetic north. The difference between these points, which varies depending on where you are on the planet, is known as magnetic declination (called magnetic variation by mariners).

Most maps are referenced to true north, not magnetic north. In the US, if you are in the Midwest, it doesn't much matter because the two are nearly the same. The agonic line, or line of zero declination, runs from northern Minnesota to southern Mississippi. But as you move toward either coast, you'll see more difference. As you move west, your compass points too far east. As you move east, it points too far west.

Declination is measured in degrees, and you must specify whether it is east or west. East declination occurs whenever the magnetic needle points too far east; west declination occurs when it points too far west. In the continental US, declination ranges from about 20° east to 20° west. In Los Angeles, it's about 14° east. In New York City, it's about 13° west. In Alaska it's even worse, exceeding 35° in some areas.

What does this mean? Let's say you're near San Francisco, with a declination of about 15° east. If your GPS receiver is set to give you a bearing referenced to true north (a "true bearing") but your compass

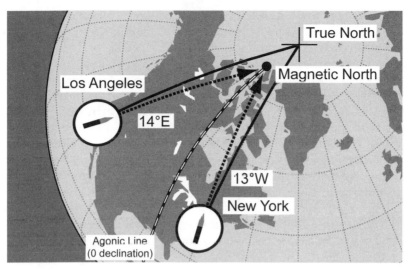

A compass points to magnetic north, not true north. The difference between the two directions is called magnetic declination.

is set to magnetic north (a "magnetic bearing"), you will think you're going in the right direction when you are really headed 15° too far east. Walk only 4 miles in this direction, and you'll have deviated a full mile from your intended path.

A good compass allows you to compensate for magnetic declination. On the left, the compass is set for zero declination. On the right, it is set for 15° east declination. Notice how the north reference indicator no longer points to 0°. On this Suunto compass, you set declination from the underside of the compass by turning the adjustment screw visible in the upper left portion of the black ring.

The same problem occurs when working with a map. If you measure a bearing from a map and then use a magnetic compass to guide you in the wilderness, you'll have to compensate for declination.

Most books at this point admonish you to memorize the mathematics used to convert true to magnetic bearings and back, with dubious mnemonics like "east is least, west is best." But I'm not going to do that. (If you really want to know how to do the math, read the sidebar on page 44.) My advice is to avoid the whole issue by buying a compass with adjustable declination and setting it to the local declination. That way, you don't have to worry about the difference.

Here's how it works: Remember that the north reference indicator on a compass vial normally points to the 0° marking on its perimeter. This means that when you center the magnetic needle inside the indicator, your compass is oriented so that 0° points to magnetic north. But you'd really like 0° to point to true north. Some compasses allow you to adjust the north reference indicator to compensate for declination. Such a compass has a separate declination scale calibrated in degrees east and west, and it allows you to change where the north reference indicator points. For example, to set your compass for 15° east declination, adjust the north reference indicator so it is pointing to 15E on the declination scale. Conversely, if you want to set it for 15° west declination, adjust the indicator to 15W on the declination scale. Some compasses provide a little screwdriver on a lanyard you can use to make the adjustment. With others, you do it by hand without any tools. Either way, once it's set, you don't have to worry about doing mental math after an exhausting 10-hour hike.

There's still the little matter of knowing the declination for your location. One way to find out is to check a recent topo map of the area.

CORRECTING FOR MAGNETIC DECLINATION

First, let me point out you shouldn't need to read this. As long as you adopt one of two sensible approaches to GPS navigation, you should never need to do mental arithmetic to correct for declination. My recommendation is to buy a magnetic compass with adjustable declination, set it to the local declination, and set your GPS receiver to display true bearings. Alternatively, you can buy an inexpensive magnetic compass without adjustable declination and set your GPS receiver to display magnetic bearings. Either way, as long as your compass and your GPS receiver are aligned, you don't have to worry about declination.

If you still want to know how to do the math, read on. The situation I will describe assumes you are using an inexpensive compass without a declination adjustment, and you have set your GPS receiver to read true bearings.

The rules are simple, if you can remember them. To convert the true bearing reported by your GPS receiver into a magnetic bearing, do the following:

▶ If your magnetic declination is east, subtract declination.

▶ If your magnetic declination is west, add declination.

This is the origin of the mnemonic "east is least, west is best." East being "least" means you subtract declination; and with a little stretch of your imagination, you can say that west being "best" means you add declination.

Magnetic declination is almost always indicated on a topo map, either graphically or in text. Or you can find it from the National Oceanic and Atmospheric Administration (NOAA) magnetic declination website, www.ngdc.noaa.gov/seg/geomag/jsp/Declination.jsp, by entering the zip code or latitude and longitude of the desired location. You can even look it up on your GPS receiver. Go to the SETUP (sometimes called SYSTEM) page and select the feature called "North Reference." Normally, it should be set to true north. But if you change the setting to MAGNETIC (sometimes called AUTO), it will show the declination of your current position to the nearest degree. Make sure you set it back to TRUE north when you are finished.

UTM GRID AND 1979 MAGNETIC NORTH DECLINATION AT CENTER OF SHEET

Declination is almost always shown on a topographic map. On USGS maps, the star indicates true north, MN indicates magnetic north, and GN indicates grid north, used only in the UTM system. Don't depend on the drawn angle to accurately represent the true declination angle.

Let's take an example: Suppose you are in southern Utah, where the magnetic declination is 13° east. Your GPS receiver tells you your destination waypoint lies at a true bearing of 155°. To convert this to a magnetic bearing, subtract 13°. This gives you a magnetic bearing of 142°.

Now suppose you are in Vermont, where the magnetic declination is 15° west. In this case, you have to add 15°. If your GPS receiver reports a true bearing of 155°, then the magnetic bearing is 170°.

If this isn't complicated enough, it gets worse. Let's suppose you're out in the wilderness and see an interesting mountain peak in the distance. You want to identify it on the map, so you take a compass reading to measure its bearing. Thanks to your GPS receiver, you know exactly where you are on the map, so you can just draw a line on the map at the correct bearing angle from your current location to see which peak it intersects. Seems simple enough.

Well, if you don't have a compass with adjustable declination, you'll be reading a magnetic bearing. But the map is aligned with true north, so you have to correct the bearing before you plot the line on the map. In this case, though, the situation is reversed. If your declination is east, you have to add declination to the compass reading to get a true bearing. If it's west, you have to subtract. It's enough to make seasoned hikers want to do all their hiking in the Midwest, where declination is close enough to zero that you don't have to worry about it.

In the continental US, magnetic declination changes only gradually as you change your position. You should easily be able to move 100 miles or more before it's different enough to worry about resetting your compass.

Magnetic declination varies over time. Over the last hundred years, the magnetic pole has moved nearly 900 miles north. In some areas, this has caused a change of more than a degree of declination every 10 years. So check the publication date of any map you use. If it's more than 10 years old, its declination information could be out of date. The information on the NOAA website is always current.

Don't forget to check the north reference setting in your receiver. There are usually several choices: TRUE bearings are referenced to true north. MAGNETIC (sometimes called AUTO) bearings are referenced to magnetic north. Your receiver uses a table stored in memory to compute magnetic declination, so after many years, it will become out of date. A third choice on some receivers (labeled USER) allows you to manually set declination. (Other choices can include such little-used favorites as GRID, MILITARY TRUE, or MILITARY MAGNETIC. As a civilian wilderness navigator, you will probably never need to worry about these.)

Over the last hundred years, the magnetic North Pole has moved nearly 900 miles northwest.

NAVIGATING BY MAGNETIC BEARINGS

This book strongly advocates the use of true bearings when navigating in the outdoors, and the use of a magnetic compass that has been adjusted for the local declination. That way, it's easy to switch between bearings read from a paper map and those shown by your GPS receiver. This is especially important if you are a serious hiker or backpacker. But sometimes you may want to use magnetic bearings. If you are traveling over long distances where declination changes significantly, it can be problematic to remember to constantly adjust it. That's why aircraft and ships navigate by magnetic bearings. Some search-and-rescue agencies also use magnetic bearings (although not all; if you are part of a SAR team coordinating a search with another agency, make sure you know what they use). And if you only have a simple compass without a declination adjustment, it is easier to use magnetic bearings.

If you choose to navigate by magnetic bearings, set your receiver to display bearings referenced to magnetic north. You can then use a simple compass and not worry about declination adjustments. The techniques described in this chapter for following a bearing work just as well with magnetic bearings as true bearings. But if you choose this approach, you'll need to remember to correct for declination if you ever use your compass to read bearings from a map.

Finding a Bearing in the Field

Now that you have adjusted your compass for your local declination, let's get back to our earlier example: You've been out in the wilderness for the afternoon and now you are ready to go back to the trailhead. You've turned on your GPS receiver and told it to go to the trailhead waypoint, which you've named something like "START." Suppose your receiver says it's 1.5 miles away at a bearing of 135°. That's great, but you still need to know what direction that is in real life.

Here's how to use a baseplate compass to find out: Rotate the compass vial so that 135° is aligned with the bearing indicator. Then hold the compass at waist level so its direction-of-travel arrow is pointing directly away from you. Now you need to orient the compass so that 0° on the vial is pointing directly north. When that happens, you know your direction-of-travel arrow is pointing to a bearing of 135°. To do this, rotate your entire body until the compass needle is boxed inside the north reference indicator on the base of the vial. Make sure you get the correct end of the needle lined up with the correct end of the north reference indicator. Otherwise, you'll head exactly opposite of your intended direction. Usually, you do this by lining up the red end of the arrow with the red end of the indicator. Check out the photo to get a better idea of the process. Once you've got the needle aligned inside the indicator, the direction-of-travel arrow points in the direction of 135°. Head in that direction for 1.5 miles, and you'll be at your car.

One word of caution when using a magnetic compass: Because it's magnetic, it can be affected by nearby metal objects. Vehicles, metal signposts, and belt buckles are common offenders. Even the batteries in your GPS receiver can have an effect. Take off your backpack and stay away from iron or steel objects when taking a compass reading.

To find a bearing in the field, set the compass vial so the desired bearing aligns with the bearing indicator. Then rotate your entire body to box the magnetic needle inside the north reference indicator. The direction-of-travel indicator now points in the desired direction. Note this compass has been adjusted for 16° east declination.

Common-Sense Navigation: Following a Bearing

Your GPS receiver can only show you the straight-line direction to your destination. It can't show you how to navigate around obstacles such as mountains, rivers, or forests. You'll rarely be able to walk a straight line in the wilderness, although something about GPS always seems to make people want to try. I can't tell you how many times I've watched otherwise sensible people, eyes glued to their receiver, go tramping through dense underbrush, poison oak, and hazardous terrain because "that's the direction my GPS told me to go." Not only is this potentially dangerous, it's a good way to harm a delicate natural environment. Ninety percent of the time, you'll be able to get to your destination primarily by following established trails. Most of the rest of the time, a little reconnaissance or advance planning will show you the most sensible route.

The best way to navigate with GPS is to do it the same way you would in the more traditional map-and-compass approach. Use your receiver to find the distance and bearing to your destination, then use your compass to see what direction that is. Look in that direction and pick a distant object like a large tree, mountain peak, or telephone pole you can use as a reference point. Then turn off your receiver and put it away. Use your eyes and brain to find the best route to get to that object.

Go around obstacles, not over the top of them. If you lose sight of your goal, pull out your receiver to get an updated bearing, then put it away. When you reach the first reference object, use your receiver to find the new bearing to your destination. Then pick out a new object in the distance and repeat the process. Keep it up until your get to your goal.

One of the most common mistakes made by novices is thinking the bearing they measured at the start of the hike is the same one they should use for the entire hike. They don't realize that unless you are moving directly toward your destination, the bearing to it will change as you move. Fortunately, with GPS, that's not a problem. Just remember to occasionally turn on your receiver and get a current update of the bearing and distance to your destination, then adjust your heading accordingly.

Summary of Simple Navigation

Now let's summarize the process of storing your present location and using your GPS receiver to return to it later.

Setup

1. Before you begin, make sure the north reference setting on your GPS receiver is set to TRUE .

2. Set the declination adjustment of your compass to your local declination. Check a recent topo map or the NOAA website if you don't know the local declination.

At the Trailhead

1. Turn on your GPS receiver and wait for it to acquire a position fix. Confirm it is operating in 3D mode, not 2D mode.

2. Decide on an easy-to-remember waypoint name such as "START" for the trailhead or "CAR" for your car. Call up your receiver's waypoint list and delete any existing waypoint with the same name.

3. To store your present location, select the MARK function. Do this by pressing the MARK button (if your receiver has one), selecting MARK from the appropriate menu page, or using the MARK shortcut (if your receiver has one).

4. When the MARK WAYPOINT page is displayed, change the waypoint name from the default number to the name you have chosen.

5. Select the command to store the waypoint. On Garmin receivers, this is usually the choice labeled OK. On Magellan receivers, it is labeled SAVE.

6. Call up the waypoint database and confirm that your
waypoint has been stored.

When Ready to Return

1. Turn on your receiver and
wait for it to acquire a position fix.

2. Select the GOTO function.
Some receivers have a dedicated GOTO button. Others
require that you use the FIND
function to choose a specific
waypoint from the database,
then select the choice labeled
GOTO.

3. On the receiver's compass
page, note the distance and
bearing to your destination.

Navigating Back to Your
Starting Point

When following a bearing, look for a feature such as a
distant mountain peak in the desired direction. Then
put your GPS receiver away and keep the feature in
sight as you hike. Take the most logical route toward
it rather than blindly following a straight line across
difficult terrain. Use your GPS receiver to update the
bearing to your destination occasionally, and select a
new feature in the distance when necessary.

1. Set your compass so the GPS
bearing to your destination is aligned with the direction-of-travel indicator.

2. Hold the compass in front of you at waist level with the direction-
of-travel arrow pointing directly away from you. Rotate your entire body until the magnetic compass needle aligns inside the north
reference indicator. The direction-of-travel indicator is now pointing
toward your destination.

3. Pick a reference point within the line of your bearing and follow the
guidelines for common-sense navigation on page 48. When you arrive at the reference point, take another bearing with your GPS and
repeat the process until you reach your destination.

For some people, this may be all you need to know about GPS navigation. If you only want to find your way back to your starting point or
store the locations of places you've already been to, you don't need to
worry about things like latitude and longitude or how to enter coordinates from a map. Knowing how to mark and go to waypoints may be
all you need. But if not, the next chapters will show you how to use a
GPS receiver in more ambitious journeys.

Part II
Navigation for the Outdoor Explorer

Key Concepts

- ▶ Basics of latitude and longitude
- ▶ Position formats and datums
- ▶ UTM grid
- ▶ How to enter waypoint coordinates into a GPS receiver
- ▶ Understanding topo maps and software maps
- ▶ Planning routes with GPS and maps

Knowing Your Position

I f you want to use GPS to do more than just return to places you've already been, you'll need to know how to enter waypoints into your receiver without actually going to them. To do this, you first need to understand latitude and longitude. Hikers and backpackers will also want to know the Universal Transverse Mercator (UTM) system, described later in this chapter. Chapter 5 will cover how to enter waypoint coordinates into your receiver.

Latitude and Longitude

You might already be familiar with the concept of latitude and longitude as a way to describe your position anywhere on earth. Originally developed by sailors to guide them across oceans, it divides the earth into lines of latitude, which indicate how far north or south of the equator you are, and lines of longitude, which indicate how far east or west of the prime meridian you are.

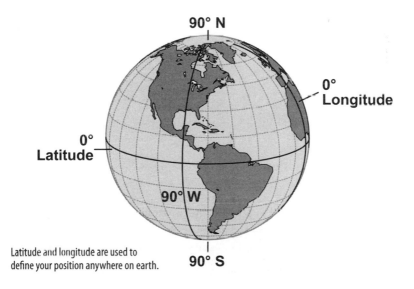

Latitude and longitude are used to define your position anywhere on earth.

The equator is defined as 0° latitude, the North Pole as 90° north latitude, and the South Pole as 90° south latitude. A complete description of latitude must always include the hemisphere—either north or south. If you just report latitude as 34° without indicating the hemisphere, you could equally be describing the latitude of Los Angeles, California, or Santiago, Chile. All locations in the US are north latitude.

Latitude lines are always parallel to the equator, so they are called parallels. They become smaller in diameter as you move north or south from the equator, but the distance between them remains the same regardless of where you are on the globe.

Longitude lines are called meridians. They are circles perpendicular to latitude that run from pole to pole. Unlike latitude, all lines of longitude are the same diameter. They are called great circles because they are the largest diameter circles you can draw around a sphere. Longitude lines all come together at the poles, so the distance between them gets smaller as you move away from the equator.

Longitude doesn't have a convenient natural reference point equivalent to the equator for latitude. So the location of 0° of longitude, called the prime meridian, is entirely arbitrary. Since the English were the dominant navigators of the 18th century, they chose to define it as the line that runs through the Royal Observatory at Greenwich, England. With only minor changes and the objections of the French notwithstanding, this definition was officially adopted at the 1884 International Meridian Conference in Washington, DC. The recalcitrant French, though, pouted for another 27 years before they grudgingly abandoned Paris as the site of their prime meridian.

Longitude is a number from 0° to 180° east or west of the prime meridian. Any individual longitude line is only half a circle that runs down one hemisphere from the North Pole to the South Pole. The other half of the same circle, running up from the South Pole to the North Pole, is different in number and opposite in hemisphere. As with latitude, don't forget to specify the hemisphere, either east or west. In the US, all lines of longitude are west longitude.

Position Formats

Let's look at how you could describe a position using latitude and longitude. For our example, we'll use the location of the famous Delicate Arch at Arches National Park in Utah. Delicate Arch is north of the equator at latitude 38 degrees, 44 minutes, 37 seconds. It is west of the prime meridian, at longitude 109 degrees, 29 minutes, 58 seconds. When describing a position, latitude comes first. You can write the hemisphere either before or after the number. Most people put it in front. Here's how it would look:

N38° 44′ 37″

W109° 29′ 58″

This is the commonly used position format known as hemisphere-degrees-minutes-seconds. It's similar to how we describe time. Each degree is divided into 60 minutes, and each minute is further subdivided into 60 seconds. A degree of latitude represents a distance of about 69 miles anywhere on earth, so 1 second of latitude represents a distance of 101 feet.

For longitude, it's not quite as simple. The distance between lines of longitude decreases as you move north or south of the equator. In the US, for example, 1 second of longitude ranges from about 87 feet in Jacksonville, Florida, to about 64 feet in Seattle, Washington. Many GPS receivers can display latitude and longitude to a tenth of a second resolution. That's a resolution of about 10 feet in latitude and, for US locations, between 6 and 9 feet in longitude.

Although the degrees-minutes-seconds format is commonly used, there are other formats, and you need to know how to tell the difference. If your friend gives you the location of a geocache in one format, for example, and you think it's in another, you'll never find it. One of the most common errors made by experts and novices alike is to incorrectly identify the latitude-longitude format of a position they have been given.

A second position format, known as hemisphere-degrees-decimal minutes, is becoming increasingly popular. It is the preferred format for reporting geocaches. In this format, the number of seconds is converted to fractional numbers of minutes. (You do this by dividing the number

Latitude and longitude of Delicate Arch, Arches National Park, Utah

of seconds by 60 and adding the result to the number of minutes.) The position of Delicate Arch in the hemisphere-degrees-decimal minutes format looks like this:

N38° 44.617′

W109° 29.967′

A third, less common position format is known as hemisphere-decimal degrees. It goes one step further and converts the number of minutes into fractions of a degree. Again, divide decimal minutes by 60 and add the result to the number of degrees. This is what the position of Delicate Arch looks like in the hemisphere-decimal degrees format:

N38.74361°

W109.49945°

If you've been given GPS coordinates from someone else or have gotten them from a book or the Internet, make sure you understand their position format. It's easy to get confused because many times the symbols for degrees, minutes, and seconds aren't written down. In that case, you have to figure it out by looking. If it is a set of three numbers separated by spaces, you know it is degrees-minutes-seconds. This is true even if the last number has a decimal point with a number after it—this is just fractions of a second. If it's a set of two numbers, the second having a decimal point and subsequent digits, you know it is the degrees-decimal minutes format. And if it's just one number with a decimal point and subsequent digits, you know it's the decimal-degrees format. To further confuse things, on some computer printouts, you'll see just a single long number of six or seven digits without any spaces or decimal points. This is a short-form method for the degrees-minutes-seconds format. Computers also often represent north and east by "+" signs and south and west by "−" signs.

Your receiver can select from among the different latitude-longitude formats, along with a number of other position formats. Here's how the different latitude-longitude choices are displayed:

Format	**Garmin**	**Magellan**	**Lowrance**
Deg-min-sec	*hddd°mm'ss.s"*	*DEG/MIN/SEC*	*Deg/Min/Sec*
Deg-dec minutes	*hddd°mm.mmm'*	*DEG/MIN/MMM*	*Degrees/Minutes*
Decimal degrees	*hddd.ddddd°*	*DEG/DDDDD*	*Degrees*

Once you select a position format, your receiver automatically converts the coordinates of any existing waypoints to the new format. But if you're entering new waypoints, you need to make sure your receiver is set to the correct position format before you begin to enter numbers. This is another very common mistake that can result in large errors.

Remember: Your receiver always assumes that any new waypoint is being entered in the currently defined position format. Once the data is entered, your receiver always maintains a waypoint at the same physical location on earth, regardless of how you later change formats. The only way to correct a mistake is to first set your receiver to the correct position format and then re-enter the data.

| Coordinate System |
| Coordinate System 1 |
| Degrees |
| **Degrees/Minutes** |
| Deg/Min/Sec |
| UTM |
| MGRS (Standard) |
| MGRS (Std.+10) |

N   36°08.971'

W   95°50.579'

[Setup Map Fix]

[Setup Loran TD]

Your GPS receiver can be configured to display coordinates in a number of formats. This is the display on the Lowrance iFinder H20c.

To drive the point home, let's go back to the example of Delicate Arch. Recall that in the degrees-minutes-seconds format, the latitude of Delicate Arch is:

N38° 44′ 37.0″

Now suppose you didn't realize your receiver was set to degrees-decimal minutes format, and you used the above data to incorrectly enter its latitude as:

N38° 44.370′

This has the same digits but it's the wrong format. (The correct value for the degrees-decimal minutes format would be N38° 44.617′.) You've just introduced an error of about 1500 feet! You can't fix the problem just by switching your receiver to the degrees-minutes-seconds format after you have entered the data. You have to first set the correct position format, then go back and edit the coordinates to the correct numbers.

The UTM Grid

All maps suffer from a common problem: They must represent the three-dimensional surface of the earth on a two-dimensional sheet of paper or computer screen. No matter how you do it, this introduces some distortion. We've all seen maps that try to portray the entire world as a single rectangular sheet, and others that cut it into oddly shaped pieces like the peels of an orange. Distortions are usually most noticeable on lines of longitude. On a three-dimensional globe, all longitude lines are straight, but when they are projected onto on the flat surface of a map, some will be straight, others bent.

As we have also seen, the distance between lines of longitude decreases as you move away from the equator. At the equator, a degree of longitude spans about 69 miles, while at the Arctic Circle, it is only about 26 miles. Latitude doesn't suffer this problem. A degree of latitude spans 69 miles (ignoring very minor variations due to the earth's slightly elliptical shape) everywhere on the globe.

This variation makes it difficult to measure latitude and longitude coordinates on a map. Special latitude-longitude rulers have been developed, but as you will see in Chapter 7, they are cumbersome to use, especially in the field. The Universal Transverse Mercator, or UTM, grid was developed as a way to make it easier to determine the coordinates of a location on a paper map. As you might imagine, it has its roots in the military, where a similar grid is known as the Military Grid Reference System, or MGRS. It is designed for use with large-scale maps such as the USGS 7.5-minute series.

Mapmakers have used many different approaches to project the three-dimensional surface of the earth onto a two-dimensional map. All introduce some level of distortion.

The UTM grid divides the entire world from 80° south latitude to 84° north latitude into 60 zones, each covering 6 degrees of longitude. The zones are numbered consecutively, with zone 1 covering the range from 180° to 174° west longitude. Subsequent zones increase in

World UTM zones

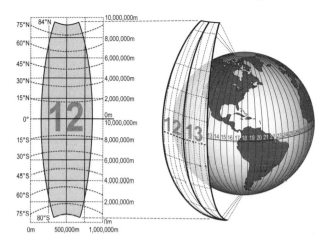

The coordinate grid for each UTM zone is completely independent from every other zone. Notice how the rectangular UTM grid for Zone 12 extends beyond the zone borders. Only the portion of the grid that lies within the zone represents valid UTM coordinates.

number every 6 degrees as you move eastward. The continental US is covered by zones 10 through 19. A rectangular metric grid overlays each zone. However, since the grid for each zone is completely independent of those in other zones, UTM is somewhat complicated to use for travels that stretch across multiple zones.

The grid for each zone is 1,000,000 meters wide, centered on the central meridian of the zone. The entire UTM grid is divided at the equator into two halves. The northern half has its origin at the equator and stretches north to 10,000,000 meters at the North Pole. The southern half is designed so that the equator is at 10,000,000 meters, with numbers decreasing to zero at the South Pole. Neither pole, however, is actually included inside the UTM system. Instead, a separate grid known as Universal Polar Stereographic, or UPS, covers the polar regions above 84° north and below 80° south. (UPS is outside the scope of this book, so if you want to learn more about it, you might try wading through the "Defense Mapping Agency Technical Manual on UTM and UPS" at earth-info.nga.mil/GandG/publications/tm8358.2/TM8358_2.pdf.)

The UTM system is designed so that you read horizontal distances eastward and vertical distances northward from reference lines. Not surprisingly, these are called eastings and northings. To measure the coordinates of a location, you first read its distance in meters east of a vertical reference line, then north of a horizontal reference line—a process often expressed as "read right, then up."

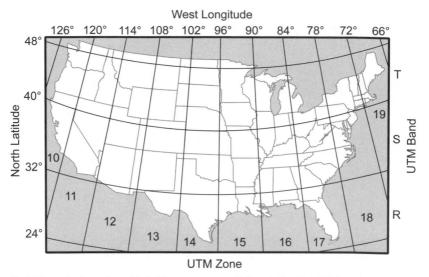

The UTM zone for the continental United States spans zones 10 through 19 and bands R through U. Each zone spans 6 degrees of longitude, and each band spans 8 degrees of latitude.

Each zone is only 6 degrees wide, which means that at the equator, its width is only about 414 miles, or 666,000 meters. Since lines of longitude converge as you move toward the poles, it gets even smaller as you move north or south from the equator. This means the rectangular UTM grid extends outside the true zone boundaries on all sides as shown in the figure on page 59. The central grid line of the zone runs straight along the longitude of its central meridian, 3 degrees away from either border. This line is arbitrarily assigned a value of 500,000 meters so that no matter where in the zone you are, you will always read a positive easting number. And since the easting boundaries lie outside the confines of the zone, there is no point in the zone with an easting of zero or 1,000,000.

For coordinates in the northern hemisphere, the northing origin is defined as the equator. But if you used this approach for the southern hemisphere, all northing measurements would be negative numbers, which is why the equator is assigned the value of 10,000,000 meters. To keep you from getting confused as to whether a particular set of coordinates refers to the northern hemisphere or southern hemisphere, each zone is divided vertically into 20 bands of latitude, each 8 degrees high. The bands are assigned letters from "C" at the extreme south to "X" at the extreme north (excluding the letters I and O, which could be confused for 1 and 0), as shown in the figure on page 58. The equator lies at the boundary between zones M and N. band X is actually 12 degrees high, an afterthought that came about when the designers realized that 8 degrees wasn't enough to cover the northernmost regions of Greenland. The full UTM coordinates for a point therefore must include the UTM zone number, the vertical band letter within the zone, and a single long number that is the combination of the easting and northing numbers, like this example:

11 S 6456673862920

The "11" means zone 11, and the "S" means vertical band S within the zone. The single long number is the combination of the easting and the northing. When there are an odd number of digits, the easting number always has one less digit than the northing. So in this example, the easting is 645667 meters and the northing is 3862920 meters. Sometimes you'll see UTM coordinates with fewer digits. This just means there is less resolution to the number. With 13 digits as in the above example, the resolution is 1 meter. With seven digits, the resolution is only 1 kilometer, as in this example:

11 S 6453862

Here, the easting is 646 kilometers and the northing is 3862 kilometers. Note that UTM coordinates are always truncated, not rounded, when they are shortened. This means that the actual UTM coordinates refer to the lower left corner of a square whose sides are the length of the resolution of the coordinates, not the center of the square. At a given coordinate resolution, every location within this square has the same coordinate value.

UTM coordinates are designed to be "read right, then up." In this example, the coordinates of Red Hill are 492838E, 4252461N. The full coordinate description must include the UTM zone number and band letter found on the map margin.

In an attempt to make it easier to read, the easting and northing numbers are often written on separate lines, like this:

11 S 0645667
3862920

That's how your GPS receiver shows the numbers. Notice the leading zero on the easting number so that both easting and northing have the same number of digits.

Sometimes you'll see UTM coordinates written on a single line with easting and northing spelled out:

11 S E645667 N3862920

This is how UTM coordinates are shown on the www.geocaching.com website, for example. Just remember the "E" and "N" are only for clarification. You don't actually enter them into your GPS receiver. And you'll probably have to enter a leading zero on the easting number.

Topo maps usually abbreviate the UTM number. Since the tic marks occur on 1000-meter increments, there's no need to show the last three zeroes except in the lower left and upper right corners. The digits representing the 1000- and 10,000-meter values are also printed in a larger font. The values in the lower left and upper right corners of the map look like this: $^6 47^{000}$m E and $^{38} 62^{000}$m N. Across the rest of the map, values are abbreviated to look like this: $^6 46$ and $^{38} 63$.

Looking at the illustration on page 59, you can see that the only place where the UTM grid exactly aligns with latitude is at the equator, and the only place it aligns with longitude is on the central meridian of the zone. Everywhere else, there is an angular offset between the two. This difference is called grid north and is usually indicated on a topo map (see the illustration on page 45). Because each zone is 6 degrees wide, the maximum deviation that can occur between grid north and true north is 3 degrees.

USGS topo maps include UTM information either in the form of tic marks on the map neatlines or as a full grid overlay. The USGS map of Half Dome on page 77 includes the full grid. Notice how the gridlines are tilted toward the west, indicating this region lies west of the zone's central meridian.

You may wonder why the UTM system incorporates so many latitude bands when it might seem sufficient to simply use two bands to indicate either "north" or "south" of the equator. In fact this would work except for a few zones in the Nordic regions of Europe. Several latitude bands there have been widened so that Norway and the Svalbard Islands can be accommodated without having to switch zones at inconvenient spots. Some software programs like National Geographic's Topo!

simplify entry of waypoints by asking only for the hemisphere, either "north" or "south," but you should never use "N" for north or "S" for south when recording a UTM waypoint, because these could be confused with the letter N and S latitude bands, both of which are in the northern hemisphere.

People who have done a lot of hiking with paper maps swear by the UTM system because it is much easier to measure UTM coordinates from a paper map than to measure latitude and longitude. This is certainly true, but UTM has its own limitations. Foremost, it really works best for short journeys that remain inside a single UTM zone. This becomes a problem when you plan a trek that cuts across more than one zone. Unfortunately for hikers in California's Sierra Nevada, the transition between zones 10 and 11 cuts right down the middle of the range in the Lake Tahoe area.

Another problem is that UTM isn't at all intuitive. If you come across UTM coordinates for an unfamiliar place, you won't have any idea where it is unless you have committed the system to memory. Take a coordinate beginning with 13T, for example. Is it in Nebraska or Arkansas? At least with latitude and longitude, you have some idea what part of the country you're talking about.

With the coming of electronic maps, the advantages of the UTM system are less pronounced. On your computer screen, it's just as easy to read latitude and longitude as it is to read UTM. And almost without exception, online and printed GPS waypoint coordinates are published as latitudes and longitudes. If you are in the military or belong to a search-and-rescue team, you'll need to know UTM. If you're a serious backpacker, you'll also want to learn it so you can more easily read coordinates from paper topo maps in the field. For the rest of us, it's probably not necessary.

Map Datum

So far, this discussion has covered navigation coordinates as if position format is your only worry. But there's another factor as well: the datum used as the horizontal reference. What's a datum? Well, think back to when you learned geography in school. You might vaguely remember your teacher saying the world is not exactly round; it's really an oval with a bulge in the middle caused by the earth's rotation. The distance from the North Pole to the center of the earth is about 6.5 miles less than it would be if the earth were a perfect sphere. This might not seem like much, but it presents a bit of a problem for latitude and longitude because they are designed for use on a true sphere. If you didn't correct for

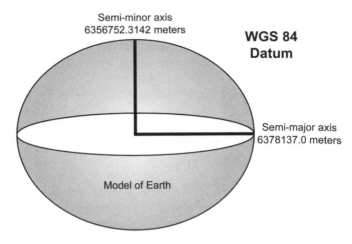

The WGS 84 datum uses an ellipsoidal model of the earth referenced to its center. The older NAD 27 uses a different reference, so the same latitude and longitude coordinates represent a different physical location.

this, then 90° north latitude would not be exactly at the North Pole, but rather at a spot in the sky 6.5 miles overhead.

A datum is a model of the earth that allows you to fit latitude and longitude onto its flattened surface. Many different datums have been used over the years by different countries. The two most important for the US are the North American Datum of 1927, known as NAD 27, and the World Geodetic Survey of 1984, known as WGS 84. These datums represent the earth as an ellipsoid, which is just a fancy name for an oval. The Global Positioning System was designed around the WGS 84 datum, but many older topographic maps use NAD 27. Always check your map to see which one it uses. The two datums use slightly different models of the earth, so coordinates expressed with reference to the WGS 84 datum can be as much as 600 feet away from the same coordinates referenced to NAD 27.

Datums are also important for UTM users, since UTM is referenced to latitude and longitude (recall that the centerline of each UTM zone aligns exactly with a degree line of longitude). Since most USGS topo maps are referenced to NAD 27, this is the datum most commonly associated with UTM coordinates. But that's not always the case, so if you have any doubt, be sure to verify the datum of your coordinates.

You should always verify the datum setting in your receiver. You'll usually find it in one of the menus under the SETUP page. There will be only one choice for WGS 84 (it may also list NAD 83, which is a virtually identical datum), but there may be many choices under NAD 27. If so, you will want the one labeled NAD 27 CO-NUS for "continental US." The other NAD 27 choices are regional variations. There will also be many other choices, with strange names like "Viti Levu 1916" and "Timbalai 1948." Unless you are an archaeologist using antiquated maps or you travel extensively outside the US, you'll probably never use most of them.

Know how to change your receiver's active map datum. On this Garmin GPSmap 60CSx, you make the selection from the SETUP menu under the UNITS submenu.

Entering
and Navigating
to Stored Waypoints

Once you understand latitude and longitude and UTM, you're ready to step up to the next level of navigation skills: programming the coordinates of a waypoint into your GPS receiver without first going to that location. This chapter assumes you have obtained the coordinates from a friend, the Internet, or another published source. If so, all you need to know is how to enter them into your receiver. Later, in Chapter 7, you will learn the more advanced technique of plotting your own course by reading coordinates from a map.

Geocaching is a typical example of the kind of navigation covered here. Geocaching websites provide the locations of thousands of caches hidden throughout the world by people like you and me. Fans of the sport log onto one of these sites and use its search tool to get a list of all the caches in their immediate area. They then record the waypoint coordinates for any sites of interest and enter them into their receiver. Much of the fun comes in using the receiver to guide them to the cache. The rest comes from discovering the prizes contained within. Geocaching is covered in more detail in Chapter 11. In this chapter, you'll see how to enter coordinates into your receiver and how to navigate more complex routes.

Obtaining Waypoint Coordinates

The first step is to obtain the coordinates of the places you want to go. For geocachers, this is easy. There are numerous websites listing the exact WGS 84 latitudes and longitudes of thousands of hidden caches. You just need to copy down the coordinates of a likely cache and enter them into your receiver.

If you're not a geocacher, you'll have to look elsewhere. Books are one possible source. Hiking guides often publish coordinates for trailside

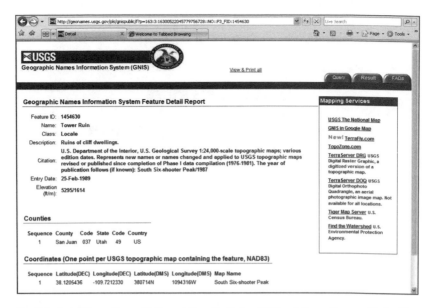

The US Geological Survey Geographic Names Information System (GNIS) website provides you with the ability to find latitude and longitude coordinates of more than 2 million physical and cultural features within the United States and its territories. The NAD 83 map datum used on this site is essentially identical to WGS 84. Note that the coordinates are displayed in the decimal degrees format.

campsites or other points of interest. The Internet can also be useful well beyond geocaching. Numerous sites give you coordinates of just about any place you can think of throughout the world. Internet sites come and go with great regularity, so rather than publishing a list here, I'll recommend two sites that will probably be around awhile.

The first page, gpsinformation.net/main/waypts-2.htm, provides links to many waypoint lists. The other is the Geographic Names Information System, or GNIS, operated by the US Geological Survey. It can give you the latitudes and longitudes for more than 2 million place names in the US and its territories. The GNIS home page is geonames.usgs.gov/index.html. From there, go to the "Domestic Names" page and then to "Search GNIS." Once you have found the name of the feature, you can click on various mapping services on the right side of the page to pull up a topo map, highway map, or aerial photo of the spot.

The map datum for the GNIS site has recently been changed from NAD 27 to NAD 83, a datum virtually identical to WGS 84. Be aware the coordinates are read from USGS 7.5-minute topo maps, so they may only be accurate to 5 seconds—about 500 feet in latitude, and a bit less in longitude.

Most waypoint coordinates you are likely to come across are reported as latitudes and longitudes, although sometimes you'll see them described in UTM (UTM is most likely to show up in hiking and backpacking magazines and guidebooks). Remember that your GPS receiver knows how to convert from UTM to latitude-longitude and back, so even if you don't understand the UTM system, you can still use it. Just set your receiver's position format to UTM and enter the number/letter combinations exactly as given. Once you've done that, you can switch your receiver back to latitude-longitude if you like.

Organizing Waypoint Coordinates

Once you have the coordinates for all the waypoints you want to program into your receiver, you need to do some basic housekeeping chores:

1. Determine the map datum for the coordinates. This will usually be either WGS 84 or NAD 27. If you have multiple waypoints with a mix of datums, group all the WGS 84 waypoints together in one set and all the NAD 27 waypoints together in a second set. If you have waypoints referenced to the NAD 83 datum, just treat them as if they were WGS 84.

2. Verify the position format for the coordinates. It will usually be either hemisphere-degrees-decimal minutes or hemisphere-degrees-minutes-seconds. Again, if you have a mix of formats, group all of one format together in one set, all the others into another set. If you have a mix of datums and position formats, you will typically have no more than four separate sets of waypoints. If your coordinates also include some in UTM and some in decimal degrees, it could be as many as eight.

3. Decide on the name you want to assign to each waypoint and write it next to its waypoint coordinates. Check to see if a waypoint of the same name already exists in the receiver's database. If so, just edit the coordinates of the existing waypoint rather than creating a new waypoint from scratch.

Programming Waypoint Coordinates

Now you're ready to enter the data into your GPS receiver. If you have multiple waypoints, the process can take awhile, so make sure the batteries in your receiver are fresh. It's not necessary to be locked onto satellites when entering waypoints, so you can do this job indoors. In fact, even if you are outside, you will save considerable battery power by setting your receiver to the GPS OFF mode (Sometimes called DEMO), a choice usually found on the SETUP page.

Before entering the data, go to your receiver's SETUP page and check the setting for both the map datum and the position format. If either of them isn't the same format as your data, make the change now. Remember, you have to correctly set your receiver before you begin entering data, otherwise you'll have to start over.

You'd think that manufacturers would make it easy to enter waypoints by providing a choice

The map datum and position format are usually accessed from the SETUP page. This receiver's position format is set to degrees-decimal minutes and its map datum to WGS 84.

labeled something like CREATE WAYPOINT. But few receivers provide such a key. Instead, you have to use the same MARK key you use to store your current position, and then remember to edit the location before you save it. The actual process varies by receiver, so study your instruction manual for specific details. The general sequence looks like this:

1. Call up the MARK page.

2. Highlight the waypoint's number and change it to the chosen name.

3. Highlight the coordinates and edit them to the correct position.

4. If your receiver allows you to select from a set of symbols, you may want to change the symbol to another choice—a tent symbol for a campsite or a car symbol for the location of your parked car, for example. The advantage of doing this is that you can later go back and delete all similar waypoints without affecting other types of waypoints.

5. Some receivers allow you to enter an elevation for the waypoint. This is not a necessary input, so unless you are sure you know it, leave it blank.

6. Store the waypoint by selecting SAVE (Magellan and DeLorme receivers), ENTER (Lowrance receivers), or OK (Garmin receivers).

The method for creating waypoints on this Garmin GPSmap 60CSx is typical of many receivers. Start by pushing the MARK button as if you were storing your current location. Then, before saving the waypoint, change the waypoint name and latitude-longitude coordinates to the desired values.

The Lowrance iFinder is one of the few receivers that provides the explicit option of creating a waypoint from scratch rather than starting from your present position.

7. Repeat the process for each additional waypoint.

If all your waypoints use the same datum and position formats, you can just enter them one after another. If not, you first need to enter those that match the receiver's current formats, then go back to the SETUP page and change the datum or position format as necessary to enter the remaining waypoints.

No matter what type of GPS receiver you own, entering waypoints directly from the front panel is so cumbersome, you'll soon want to find an easier way. If you own a computer, you can make the job much easier.

All you need is the right software package. In addition to the mapping software programs discussed in Chapter 6, you can use EasyGPS, a free program you can download from the TopoGrafix website at www. easygps.com. The free version gives rather limited capability, with restricted datum and coordinate choices. Purchasing the ExpertGPS upgrade gives you many additional features.

Navigating to Stored Waypoints

You navigate to a manually programmed waypoint using the same approach as described in Chapter 3. First select the GOTO function to find the bearing and distance to the waypoint. Then use your compass to determine where that direction actually is. Finally, head in the indicated direction.

The same cautions also apply: Don't blindly head straight across uncertain terrain. Instead, pick a route that gets you in the general direction without undue risk or damage to the environment. Go around obstacles, not over them. Check your receiver occasionally to get an updated bearing, and adjust your course accordingly. And keep your eyes focused on your surroundings, not your receiver. Pick a target object like a tree or boulder in the distance and use it as an intermediate goal. When you get to it, use your receiver to update the bearing to your destination and continue the process until you arrive. If you're not sure how to follow a bearing, go back and read Chapter 3 in detail.

One added complication is that you often won't have a good idea of where your target waypoint is actually located. If it's a hidden geocache, for instance, you might not even know exactly where to park your car before beginning your search. More than once, I've parked at what I thought was a good starting point, only to find my way blocked by fence lines, cliffs, or rows of houses. So it's a good idea to at least get a general idea of the waypoint's location before you start out.

There are several ways to do this. If you own a highway or

If you have a mapping receiver, you can use its internal map to get some idea of a destination's location. The built-in base map probably won't be sufficient; you'll need to download a more detailed map from software sold by the receiver's manufacturer. This Garmin Rino has been loaded with data from the MapSource Topo software. No map is without error. The correct name of the lake shown on this map is Ilsanjo.

topographic mapping software program that runs on a personal computer, you can enter the waypoint coordinates from the keyboard and view its location on the map display. Zoom in to get a reasonable idea of how to get to the waypoint. Chapters 6 and 7 cover the subject of software maps in detail.

Another option is to use an online mapping service. Two good free sources are TopoZone at www.topozone.com and Maptech at mapserver. maptech.com/homepage/index.cfm. You'll learn more about TopoZone in Chapter 11. With Maptech, select the "Advanced Search" option and enter the waypoint coordinates in either degrees-minutes-seconds or decimal degrees. If using decimal degrees, make sure to enter a "-" sign in front of longitude to represent the western hemisphere. The result will be a digital USGS 7.5-minute map of the general area, but the desired spot won't necessarily be at the center of the page. Move the cursor while watching the latitude-longitude displays until it is over the desired position. You can also change the drop-down menu to use UTM coordinates, if you prefer.

The Maptech server uses the NAD 27 format, so if your waypoints are referenced to WGS 84, you need to convert them. This is easy enough to do. Just enter them into your receiver in WGS 84 format, and then change the receiver's map datum to NAD 27. The coordinates of your waypoints will now be displayed in NAD 27 format. Be sure to set the datum back to WGS 84 when finished.

The free EasyGPS program described here also has the ability to link directly to the TopoZone server. It places a crosshair at the waypoint's location on the online map.

Finally, you have the tried-and-true option of using paper maps. You'll need one with a latitude and longitude scale or UTM grid such as a USGS topo map. It's a little more difficult to get an accurate reading from a paper map, but you can easily get a general idea just by looking. Often, that's enough to get you to a good starting point. For more precise information, see Chapter 7, which covers the subject of route planning with paper maps.

Topographic Maps

Before you can do any serious GPS navigation, you need to understand maps. With the right map you can:

▶ See how to drive to the trailhead

▶ Plot a course across the land, either along trails or by cross-country bushwhacking

▶ Find the latitude and longitude or UTM coordinates of places you want to visit

▶ Learn the steepness and variability of the terrain you'll be crossing

▶ Identify obstacles such as rivers or cliffs along your path

▶ Find your position in the field by comparing physical features of the land to their representations on the map

Not every map is equally useful. The highway maps you pick up at the local supermarket or auto club are examples of what are called planimetric maps. They show towns and highways, and perhaps an occasional railroad or river. But they don't show terrain in any detail at all. Sometimes they plot forests in green or deserts in brown, and occasionally they will show the location and elevation of a notable mountain

Compare this USGS aerial photograph (actually a composite of two photos) of the region around Junction Butte in Canyonlands National Park, Utah, to the portion of the USGS 1:100,000 topo map for the same location. This is the same region pictured in the photo introducing Part II, taken from a point off the lower right edge of the map. (Images courtesy of the US Geological Survey) peak. But beyond this, you can't tell whether a region is dead flat or steep and mountainous. Nor can you read the latitude and longitude of a location. Highway maps are great for showing you how to drive to the trailhead, but they are nearly useless once you are actually on the trail. What you need in the wilderness is a topographic map.

USGS Maps

Topographic, or "topo," maps are produced by various government agencies and some private companies. The most comprehensive source is the US Geological Survey (USGS). USGS maps are available at USGS regional field offices as well as at many outdoor shops. You can also order them online directly from the USGS website at topomaps.usgs.gov.

The USGS produces several map series at various scales. The most comprehensive is known as the 7.5-minute series because each map covers 7.5 minutes of latitude by 7.5 minutes of longitude. This is the most useful scale for outdoor recreation. It takes about 54,000 maps to cover the entire US, including Hawaii but excluding Alaska, which uses 15-minute maps. The scale for 7.5-minute maps is 1:24,000, which means that 1 inch on the map represents 24,000 inches, or 2000 feet, in real life. (A few use a scale of 1:25,000.) These are known as large-scale maps because they cover a small area (less than 10-by-10 square miles) in great detail. It might sound counterintuitive to call a map "large scale" when it covers a small area, but that's the way it's done. Think of it as large scale because it takes a large sheet of paper to show the same area as a small-scale map shows on a small sheet.

USGS also produces topo maps at several smaller scales, including 1:100,000, 1:250,000, 1:500,000, and 1:1,000,000. These show larger areas but in less detail than the 7.5-minute series. The USGS used to produce a series of 15-minute maps, but ongoing budget pressures caused these to be discontinued ("abandoned" in USGS parlance, as if they were left off at a homeless shelter somewhere). Today, 15-minute maps are only produced for Alaska.

Fifteen-minute maps of the continental US were drawn at a scale of 1:62,500, where 1 inch represented not quite 1 mile. Not until Alaska did the USGS settle on the more practical scale of 1:63,360, which looks like a strange number but results in a map where 1 inch represents exactly 1 mile.

Fifteen-minute maps were a convenient scale for hikers, but less useful for mining and oil exploration, so when cuts had to be made, it was the 15-minute series that was abandoned. Several private companies sell updated versions of the old 15-minute series for national parks and other popular hiking areas, although they don't always print them at

Example of USGS 7.5-minute topographic map

the standard scale. Remember that USGS maps are often 10 or more years old, so don't depend on them in areas that have seen recent development. You can learn more about USGS topo maps online at erg.usgs. gov/isb/pubs/booklets/usgsmaps/usgsmaps.html.

Topo Map Basics

A topo map not only shows natural and manmade features in more detail than a planimetric map, it also displays the physical shape of the terrain. It does this by way of contour lines representing paths of constant elevation of the land. Knowing the contours of the terrain, you can determine whether your intended route is relatively flat or will climb 2000 feet. You can also determine how the route changes in elevation—a path that repeatedly climbs and descends 100 feet at a time can be more strenuous than one that slowly but steadily climbs the same amount in a single run.

Contour Lines

Most topo maps show contour lines in brown ink. To make them easier to read, every fifth line, called an index contour, is printed in bold and its elevation is labeled. Make sure you know whether the numbers are in feet or meters.

You might find it helpful to understand the concept of contour lines by thinking of an egg slicer—that handy kitchen gadget used to cut eggs, grapes, strawberries, and the occasional finger into neat stacks of slices all the same thickness. Imagine a gigantic egg slicer, its cutting wires spaced 40 feet apart, turned sideways so it can slice horizontally through a mountain. If you looked from the top down after it was sliced, the outline of the mountain at each cut would represent its contour at that elevation.

Depending on the steepness of the terrain, you might want to change the distance between the cutting wires on your giant egg slicer. In relatively flat areas, 40 feet might not give you enough resolution, so you would want to set the wires only 10 or 20 feet apart. In very steep areas, you might want an even greater spacing, perhaps 60 or 80 feet.

In the same way, the contour interval chosen by a mapmaker will depend on the local topography of the land. Maps covering mountainous areas adopt larger contour intervals than those covering fairly flat regions. You'll always find the contour interval printed somewhere on the map, usually near its scale rule. Pay attention, because it's not always the same even among different maps from the same series. Some USGS maps, for example, report contour intervals in feet, while others are in meters.

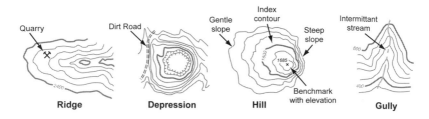

Examples of contour lines and other features found on a topographic map

By studying the shapes of the contour lines, you can learn information about the land. Lines that are close together represent steep slopes. Widely spaced lines are gentle slopes. Mountain peaks are represented by concentric rings. V-shaped lines pointing uphill indicate a canyon or gully. V- or U-shaped lines pointing downhill indicate a ridge. To help you interpret the various symbols on a topo map, the USGS produces a handy pamphlet entitled "Topographic Map Symbols." You can get an online copy at erg.usgs.gov/isb/pubs/booklets/symbols.

Practice reading topo maps by picking up a map of a nearby area. Study the map, then take it along and go out to see how it relates to the physical features of the landscape.

Elevation

Topo maps represent elevation with respect to something called a vertical datum, which is the "zero elevation" reference. Usually, this is defined as mean sea level, abbreviated MSL. Seems simple enough, right? Unfortunately, it's not. When you are at the beach, you can easily measure sea level, but if you're at a peak in the Rocky Mountains, you don't have that luxury.

There are two ways to define MSL when you don't have an ocean conveniently located nearby. The first is to define it as the elevation at which the force of gravity is the same as at actual sea level—where sea level would be if the land wasn't in the way. This is the definition used by topo maps. This line of constant gravity, called the geoid, is not a flat surface. It varies irregularly, depending on the shape of the land and the density of the rocks in the immediate vicinity. The change in local gravity caused by the mass of the mountains actually makes mean sea level higher than it would be if the mountains weren't there.

The other way to define mean sea level is to mathematically model it. Most models represent the earth as an ellipsoid. In this case, MSL is the height of the ellipsoid that best matches the true shape of the earth.

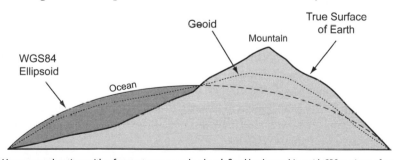

Maps report elevations with reference to mean sea level as defined by the earth's geoid. GPS receivers often measure elevation with respect to the WGS 84 ellipsoid, which only approximates mean sea level.

The standard ellipsoid adopted by GPS is the WGS 84 vertical datum. (Latitude and longitude reference the WGS 84 horizontal datum). Mathematical models are convenient for GPS receivers, but they only approximately represent the true geoid. Depending on your location, there can be a difference of more than 300 feet between the two. Across the continental US, the geoid ranges from about 10 feet above to 100 feet below the WGS 84 ellipsoid.

The scientific community has only recently spent much time trying to understand the earth's geoid. The most current geoid of the continental US is known as GEOID03. It is based on millions of gravimetric measurements made across the country. Expensive commercial GPS receivers use GEOID03 as their elevation reference, but consumer units often still use the less complicated but also less accurate WGS 84 ellipsoid. This is one reason why GPS elevation accuracy is worse than horizontal accuracy. You can learn more about GEOID03 by visiting the NOAA web page at www.ngs.noaa.gov/GEOID/GEOID03.

Understanding Topo Maps

While the "Topographic Map Symbols" pamphlet will help you understand much about the map, it won't tell you everything. Map borders are full of information of varying usefulness. Let's look at the most important information on a USGS 7.5-minute paper map.

Lower right margin. This is where you find the name of the map and its date of publication. There's also a simple legend limited to road symbols. Newer printings include an ISBN bar code.

Lower center margin. Here is the map scale, contour interval, and the vertical datum reference. Don't confuse the vertical datum, used only as an elevation reference, with the much more important horizontal datum (see below), which is used as the position reference. Coastal maps also include depth and shoreline information.

Lower left margin. Buried among such things as hydrographic data and grid tick information is the all-important horizontal datum. On most USGS maps, this is the 1927 North American Datum, or NAD 27. Although it doesn't say so, maps of the continental US use what GPS receivers often call NAD 27 CONUS, whose reference point is a physical location on the Meades Ranch in Kansas. Some newer maps also give instructions on how to translate coordinates to the NAD 83 datum, which is virtually identical to WGS 84.

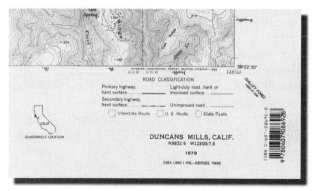

Information on a USGS 7.5-minute topographic map: lower left margin (top), lower center margin (middle), lower right margin (bottom)

Neatlines. The borders of the map, called neatlines, always align with either an even minute or a 30-second line of latitude or longitude. Along the neatlines are numbers relating to various coordinate systems. Latitude and longitude are shown in degrees-minutes-seconds format. The full numbers are printed at the map corners, but only the minutes and seconds are listed in between. Numbers for other coordinate systems are interspersed along the neatlines, making it a little difficult to identify the intermediate latitude and longitude markings. Look for the numbers with the minutes (') or seconds (") marks after them.

You can read the latitude and longitude of any point using the technique described in the next chapter, and then enter the coordinates into your receiver as a GPS waypoint. If you do this very often, though, you'll probably want to learn the UTM system, because UTM coordinates are much easier to read from a paper map. USGS maps all include blue UTM tic marks along the neatlines, and some maps have full UTM grids printed in blue. You can recognize UTM labels because the leading one or two digits are printed in smaller font than the next two digits.

The remaining black tic marks represent the State Plane Coordinate System. Only the marks nearest the lower left and upper right corners are labeled, with a number in feet. Don't worry about these markings. Unless you are a surveyor, you will have little need for them.

Finally, the names of the eight adjacent maps are centered along the vertical and horizontal neatlines and diagonally in each of the four corners of the map.

Software Maps

There are several problems with paper maps. First, each map only covers a limited area, so if your journey takes you any distance, you'll have to carry several maps. Second, it's not all that easy to read latitude and longitude coordinates from the map. Nor can you easily determine the exact elevation profile of your planned journey. Will it be a steady climb, or filled with hills and dales? After a bit of practice studying paper maps, you'll get better at interpreting elevation variations, but it will still take you considerable effort for a hike of any distance. All of these problems can be overcome through the use of software maps.

Today, there are many types of software maps. Most are designed to run on Windows PCs, while a few also have Mac versions. Some, like Garmin's MapSource (www.garmin.com), DeLorme's TopoUSA (delorme.com), or Magellan's MapSend (www.magellangps.com), are designed to load maps directly into compatible GPS receivers. These programs not only let you work from a PC, they also display detailed maps of a region directly on your GPS receiver's screen (albeit on a very small one). Each company uses a proprietary communications protocol that only works with their own receivers.

Other programs are designed to run strictly on a personal computer, but they allow you to transfer waypoints to your GPS receiver by way of a serial or USB cable. These programs work with a wide variety of receivers from many manufacturers, but since they require a computer, they

Software maps such as this one from National Geographic Topo! allow you to plan your route and see its elevation profile. (Map created with Topo! ©2006 National Geographic)

are not practical to carry in the field. They are best used to plan your route ahead of time and then print out a customized topo map for the specific region of your planned travel.

As with paper maps, software maps fall into two major categories: planimetric and topographic. Planimetric map software, designed for highway navigation, provides detailed information about roads, freeway exits, and highway mileage. Some can even use voice commands to guide you to exact street addresses. DeLorme's Street Atlas USA is a well-known example. Garmin's MapSource City Navigator and Magellan's MapSend DirectRoute also fit into this category. As with paper maps, this type of program is great for getting you to the trailhead but of limited use once you are on the trail. You'll learn a bit more about these maps in Chapter 14.

Topographic map software is much more useful for an actual hike. One type of program starts with scanned versions of USGS topo maps. These are known as raster-graphics maps because of the way the map is digitized. When viewed on the computer screen, the display looks just like a digital version of a paper topo map.

The two most widely used raster graphics programs are Topo! from National Geographic (maps.nationalgeographic.com/topo) and Terrain Navigator from Maptech (www.maptech.com). Both companies offer seamless map coverage of entire states or major recreation areas at resolutions down to the USGS 7.5-minute scale, meaning you don't have to struggle to piece together data from separate paper maps. Both also allow you to measure elevation profiles derived from the USGS digital elevation model (DEM) for each map, making it easy to determine how difficult the hike will be. And both interface with a wide variety of GPS receivers. You can create waypoints and routes in software and automatically upload them to your receiver without having to laboriously enter data by pushing multiple buttons on your receiver. You can also download stored waypoints and tracks from your receiver into the software program so you can see precisely where you have traveled. Chapter 7 explores raster-graphics mapping software in more detail.

Another type of program uses what's known as a vector graphics map. Rather than starting from scanned images of paper maps, it stores the shapes of the terrain contours, roads, and rivers as digital lines. This approach greatly reduces the memory required to store a given geography and makes it easier to provide enhanced graphics such as 3D shading, but you may lose other information typically shown on a USGS map. Artificial features such as buildings and trails could be missing or even misplaced.

Vector graphics programs offer a similar suite of functions as raster-graphics programs. You can create and download waypoints and routes, plot elevation profiles, and transfer data from your GPS receiver into the software program. The efficiency of this type of program is demonstrated by the fact that you can purchase vector-based topo software for the whole US for about the same price as a raster-based program for a single state. DeLorme's TopoUSA is the most popular vector graphics mapping program currently available. It can also create turn-by-turn driving instructions on the PC. Garmin's MapSource Topo and Magellan's MapSend Topo are two other examples, although they don't offer turn-by-turn highway navigation.

If you spend any time browsing Internet newsgroups, you'll find strong support for two other programs: OziExplorer (www.oziexplorer. com) and Fugawi Global Navigator (www.fugawi.com/web). These are both very flexible programs that allow you to work with scanned maps from any source. Load any digitized raster-graphics map into the program, calibrate it by entering the datum and the coordinates of several map locations, and the program does the rest. You can download waypoints and track logs from your GPS receiver to the computer or upload them from the computer to your receiver. Both programs provide a variety of advanced features.

OziExplorer and Fugawi are different from other programs in that they work with virtually any digitized raster-graphics map. With the right maps, they can work worldwide; products such as Terrain Navigator, Topo!, or TopoUSA provide only limited geographical coverage. But this strength is also their weakness. Terrain Navigator, Topo!, and TopoUSA are complete, turnkey systems that include both maps and

Compare these views of Yosemite Valley as shown on a raster graphics map (above) and a vector graphics map (below). National Geographic's Topo! software uses scanned versions of USGS paper maps. DeLorme's TopoUSA uses a digital representation of contour lines and map features. (Maps created with Topo! ©2006 National Geographic and TopoUSA ©2007 DeLorme. Reprinted with permission.)

software interface. Load the program into your computer and you are immediately ready to go. Neither OziExplorer nor Fugawi include maps—you have to obtain them separately. Some are available from the two companies, and there are many online sites where you can obtain free or low-cost maps. If you have access to a scanner, you can even make your own. If you are technically inclined and comfortable with the Internet, you may find OziExplorer or Fugawi to be the perfect choice. If you just want to get up and running quickly, stick to a turnkey product.

Physical Connections and Interface Protocols

The final thing you'll need to understand about connecting your GPS receiver to a personal computer is the actual physical connection and interface protocol. Newer receivers (those introduced within the last couple of years) connect to a personal computer through the USB interface. This is a fast, efficient way to transfer maps and data. Older receivers used a nine-pin serial connection known as an RS-232 port. This connector historically came standard with PCs, but has long since disappeared from newer computers. Owners of older GPS receivers with new computers will either have to install a third-party serial card or try to use an external USB-to-serial adapter. Before trying the latter approach, check with the manufacturer of your GPS receiver, as not all adapters seem to work. Garmin offers a USB-to-RS-232 cable designed to work with their receivers.

Even after you've made a good physical connection between the receiver and the computer, you still need to make sure the two are speaking the same software language. It's the equivalent of two people having a conversation in which one person is speaking French and the other is using English. Unless they both understand both languages, the conversation will be very difficult. If your receiver has a USB interface and your computer software program can communicate through USB, the job is easy. Just connect your receiver, launch the software program, and you're up and running.

The problem is a bit more complicated if your receiver doesn't have a USB interface or if you're using an older software mapping program that can't communicate through USB. In this case, you have to use the dreaded RS-232 serial connection. The industry standard for RS-232 communication between GPS and computer is known as NMEA 0183. Developed by the National Marine Electronics Association (www.nmea.org), it defines the formats for messages between the two units. The current version of the standard is 3.01, issued in January of 2002, but your receiver and mapping software should support older versions as well, specifically versions 1.5, 2.1, or 2.3. Both Magellan and Garmin support versions of this standard. Garmin also provides additional proprietary capability, not surprisingly called the Garmin interface protocol. It is supported by most third-party software programs and in most software, it is the preferred interface for use with Garmin receivers.

One last word of caution: Some receivers designed primarily for marine navigation offer the NMEA 0183 interface, but it is designed to work only with nautical equipment such as autopilots. It won't transfer user data such as waypoints or tracks to a computer. The Lowrance iFinder GO is an example of this type of receiver. Most other iFinder models are compatible with a PC through the removable MMC card.

Route Planning and Navigation

To get the most benefit from your GPS receiver, you need to know how to use it to navigate routes that include intermediate destinations along the way. It's the equivalent of going out for an afternoon of errands: You plan to stop at the post office to buy some stamps, then on to the hardware store and the gym before finishing up at the grocery store and returning home. If you've lived in the area for awhile, you can make the trip by memory. But what if you're new in town? You'll probably want to check a map and plan your itinerary. You wouldn't want to go to the grocery store first, leaving your ice cream to melt while you get in a workout at the gym.

GPS Routes

A GPS route is a similar concept. You first enter a series of waypoints, then tell your receiver the sequence you want to travel to them. When you activate the ROUTE function, your receiver automatically guides you to the first destination, just as if you had used the GOTO function. When you get there, it automatically switches to guide you to the next waypoint. It continues for each waypoint in succession until you arrive at your final destination.

Think of a route as a series of GOTO functions programmed to occur one after the other. There's nothing you can do with a route you couldn't also do by manually using the GOTO function for one waypoint after another. The advantage of the ROUTE function is that it automates the navigation process. You don't need to memorize the names of a dozen or more waypoints and the order in which you want to reach them. You can also use a route over again without having to check your notes or remember waypoint lists. And most receivers allow you to reverse a route so you can easily get back to where you started.

The important thing is to know what a route is and how to follow it. It's not absolutely necessary to use the actual ROUTE function in your

Open-loop route (left) and closed-loop route (right)

receiver—some expert navigators never use anything more than the GOTO function—but if you intend to do any serious wilderness navigation, it is critical that you at least understand how to construct and follow a multileg route. And if you know this, you might as well learn how to use the ROUTE function.

Types of Routes

There are two kinds of routes: open loop and closed loop. An open-loop route is one that goes from a starting point to a destination, traveling through intermediate points along the way. To get back to the starting point, you simply follow the route in reverse, a technique known as reversing the route.

A closed-loop route goes from a starting point, through a series of intermediate destinations, and ends up back at the starting point without reversing. The afternoon of errands described at the beginning of the chapter is an example of a closed-loop route—you don't need to return via the hardware store and post office just to get back home.

Your GPS receiver can handle either type of route interchangeably. In fact, it doesn't even know or care whether the route is open loop or closed loop. It just knows to guide you to a series of waypoints in the order you have told it. It's only important for you to know if it is an open-loop route so you know if you need to reverse the route when you reach the end.

Planning a Route with Paper Maps

An example of an open-loop route is the trail to the top of Half Dome in Yosemite National Park. First, let's review the route as shown on the map: Starting at the Happy Isles Trailhead, follow the Mist Trail to the top of Vernal Fall, then continue on to the top of Nevada Fall. There, join the John Muir Trail to its intersection with the Half Dome Trail. Turn north, taking the Half Dome Trail all the way to the peak. You don't want to get confused by various other trails that enter and depart along the way, so you can define a "route" consisting of the trails and the key intersections along the way. Of course, you will eventually want to get back to where you started, but you can do this simply by reversing the route. So your "route" only needs to define the first half of the journey.

To plan the route using USGS 7.5-minute paper maps, you need two maps, *Half Dome, CA* and *Yosemite Falls, CA*. Immediately, you discover the first problem with paper maps: All but a very small part of the trail is on the *Half Dome* map, but you need both maps to see your entire route. The part missing from *Half Dome* is so small, you probably don't want to carry the *Yosemite Falls* map on your hike. But you still need it during the planning process so you can at least be familiar with that part of the trail. (You might even want to cut and paste the small portion of the *Yosemite Falls* map onto the *Half Dome* map you carry on the hike.)

First, trace out your route on the map using a pencil or highlighter pen. Then look for the important trail junctions and other points of interest—anything that will help you stay on the right path or lead you to something you want to see. These are the locations you will program into your receiver as GPS waypoints.

Detail from the USGS 7.5-minute topo maps *Half Dome, CA,* and *Yosemite Falls, CA,* showing the trail to Half Dome and possible waypoint locations and names. The dashed line indicates the transition between the two maps. (Map created with Topo! ©2006 National Geographic)

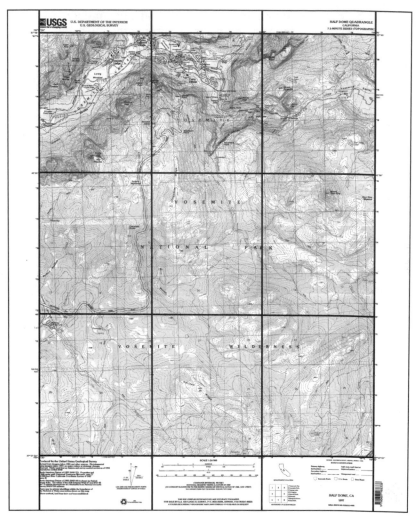

USGS 7.5-minute map *Half Dome, CA,* showing ruled lines necessary to read latitude and longitude

The map on page 90 shows seven waypoints, including the starting and ending points. This amounts to a waypoint roughly every mile, which is a reasonable interval. Of course, you should pick waypoints based on how they will help you navigate rather than simply choosing a fixed interval between them. The example waypoints represent trail junctions where there's some risk you might make a wrong turn.

For each waypoint, draw a crosshair centered on it. This makes it easier to accurately read latitude and longitude. Then give the waypoint a name. You will program this name into your GPS receiver, so make sure it fits within the receiver's naming limitations. Some receivers accept waypoint names only up to six characters long; others accept 12 or more characters. Even if they do, shorter names are usually better, especially when using a mapping receiver. You don't want the small map display cluttered with long waypoint names.

Reading Waypoint Coordinates I: Latitude-Longitude

Now comes the challenging part: determining the waypoint coordinates. In this example, you'll see how to measure latitude and longitude, although you could also easily use UTM; the 1997 edition of *Half Dome, CA* has a full UTM grid printed on it. You will learn how to use UTM in the next section.

To read latitude and longitude, you need a special latitude-longitude ruler. You can get a nice plastic one at an outdoor specialty shop, or you can photocopy the one on page 92. Before using it, you need to prepare the map by drawing ruled lines at the 2.5-minute points. Look for the 2.5-minute tic marks along the map neatlines. (There are also crosshairs within the map where these latitude and longitude lines intersect.) Lay down a yardstick and carefully draw lines to connect the corresponding marks on each side of the map. For longitude, extend the lines all the way to the edge of the paper. Do this for both the interior 2.5-minute lines and the longitude neatlines. (For latitude, you don't need to extend the lines beyond the neatlines.) When finished, your map should look similar to the one in the illustration on page 90.

Reading latitude is fairly simple. Align the ends of the latitude scale with the 2.5-minute lines on either side of the point you want to measure, making sure the north end of the scale is oriented toward the top of the map. You might need to angle the scale slightly so the two ends align exactly with the 2.5-minute lines. Reading upward from the bottom, the scale shows the incremental latitude in minutes and seconds you must add to the absolute latitude of the lower 2.5-minute line. If your waypoint doesn't align exactly with a line on the ruler, try to estimate its position to the nearest tenth of a second.

Notice the scale has two sets of numbers, one beginning with 0, and one beginning with 30. Which set you use depends on the latitude of the lower 2.5-minute line. If it is on an even minute of latitude, use the scale beginning with 0. If it is on a 30-second increment, use the scale beginning with 30. Starting from the latitude at the bottom of your ruler, find the complete latitude of your waypoint by adding the incremental minutes and seconds between this lower latitude line and your waypoint (see the upper figure on the left on page 93). Reading longitude is only

A latitude-longitude ruler (right) and a UTM roamer (above) enable you to read coordinates from a paper map. The ones shown here, which you can photocopy for your own use, are for USGS 7.5-minute maps. Read the text for instructions on their use. You can purchase more sophisticated rulers with markings for many different map scales from a good outdoor specialty shop.

slightly more complicated. Remember that the distance between lines of longitude decreases as you move away from the equator, so it's not possible to construct a fixed-length scale that's right for all maps. But there's still a way. Just tilt the ruler as shown in the illustration (see upper-right figure on page 93) until both ends align with the 2.5-minute longitude lines, making sure the east end of the scale is on the right. Keeping the scale at this angle, slide it up or down until you can read the longitude of the point of interest. Using the same process as described for latitude, add the seconds and minutes of the longitude coordinate to the longitude of the right edge of the ruler. Repeat this process for all the rest of the waypoints you have identified.

Read latitude (left) by orienting the ruler so the latitude scale aligns with the 2.5-minute lines. (You may have to tilt the ruler slightly.) Orient the scale so the north indicator points up. Add the incremental latitude of the ruler to the absolute latitude of the lower line. In this example, the lower line is on a 30-second increment, so you use the scale beginning with 30.

Read longitude (right) by tilting the ruler so the ends of the longitude scale align with the ruled 2.5-minute longitude lines. Be sure to orient the scale so the east indicator points to the right. Add the incremental longitude of the ruler to the absolute longitude of the line at the right. In this example, the right line is on an even minute of longitude, so you use the scale beginning with 0.

Reading Waypoint Coordinates II: UTM

After trying to read latitude-longitude coordinates on a paper map, you will quickly come to appreciate the UTM system. With UTM, you don't need to spread your map out on the ground and tilt a ruler at a crazy angle. You can keep it neatly folded and make your measurements using a small tool called a UTM roamer. Outdoor specialty shops sell plastic roamers calibrated for various map scales, and some compasses even have roamers printed on their baseplates. If you're using USGS 7.5-minute topo maps, you can copy and use the one on page 92 (it works best if you copy it onto transparency material).

Some USGS 7.5-minute maps—like Yosemite's *Half Dome, CA*—come with a full UTM grid preprinted on them, making it easy to read coordinates with your roamer. Others only have UTM northing and easting

1. Align corner of roamer to feature being measured

3. Add incremental northing value to bottom baseline to get: 4180310

2. Add incremental easting value to left baseline to get: 278772

4. Add UTM zone from map margin to get full coordinates:
11 S 0278772
4180310

To read UTM coordinates, place the roamer on the map so its top right corner aligns with the desired location. Add the incremental easting and northing values from the roamer to the absolute values from the map, as shown.

tic marks printed on the neatlines. If yours doesn't have the full grid, you will need to create one by drawing lines to connect the tic marks. The UTM tic marks are easy to recognize because the first digit of the northing and the first two digits of the easting are printed in a smaller font than the next two digits. Lay a yardstick so it connects the same numbers on either side of the map and use a pencil or fine-tipped pen to draw the connecting lines. (The UTM grid will not be parallel to the neatlines unless the region covered by your map lies near the central meridian of the UTM zone.) When you are finished, your map should look something like the one on page 77.

Now you are ready to read the UTM coordinates of your waypoints. Lay the roamer on the map so that its upper right corner aligns with the waypoint of interest, as shown in the diagram. Make sure the roamer is oriented parallel to the UTM gridlines, not the map neatlines. To read the coordinates, remember the adage, "read right, then up." This means you read the easting first. Write down the easting value of the map gridline at the left of the waypoint, remembering to append three zeroes to the end. Then read the incremental easting on the roamer where it intersects the gridline. (You will have to estimate the last digit by interpolating between the scale markings on the roamer.) Add this number to that of the gridline.

In the diagram, the easting of the gridline is ²78. Append three zeroes to get the number 278000. Since UTM coordinates are expressed in meters, this represents the number of meters east of the zero reference point of the zone (Refer to the illustration on page 59 if you need to review the concepts of the UTM system).

Now read the incremental easting of the roamer. In the diagram above, it is 772. Add this to the easting of the gridline to get an easting of 278772 for the waypoint. Your GPS receiver will probably want you to add a leading zero to make it 0278772.

Northing values are read similarly, working upward from the reference gridline. In the diagram on page 94, the northing of the gridline is ⁴¹80 (note that northings have one more digit than eastings). Append three zeroes to get a northing of 4180000. This is the number of meters the gridline lies north of the equator. Now read the incremental northing on the roamer, 310. Add this to the northing of the gridline to get a northing of 4180310 for the waypoint.

The complete coordinates must include the UTM zone. On a USGS topo map, this is listed in the lower left corner; the *Half Dome, CA* map is UTM zone 11. Curiously, the USGS doesn't list the alphabetical latitude band, which happens to be "S" for Yosemite. But don't worry. All you have to know is whether you are north or south of the equator. Then just enter the coordinates, and your GPS receiver will automatically determine the correct letter. (Some models don't even let you enter a latitude band, and the ones that do will automatically correct it if you get it wrong.) The full UTM coordinates then become:

11 S 0278772
4180310

Since UTM coordinates are expressed in meters, it's easy to use your roamer to measure distances between points on the map. The full length of the scale is 1000 meters, and each minor scale division represents 10 meters. You can interpolate between these minor divisions to read the coordinates of a waypoint to an accuracy of about 5 meters.

Creating the Route

Once you've measured all the waypoints, you're ready to create the route. First, enter the coordinates of each waypoint, making sure the map datum and position format are set properly (in this example, they are NAD 27 and either degrees-minutes-seconds or UTM). Now you're ready to create the route.

The details of how to do this vary, depending on your receiver, so you'll need to read your instruction manual for specific directions. In general, the sequence goes something like this:

This is the route screen on the Magellan eXplorist 200. As with all receivers, the indicated straight-line distances between waypoints may be significantly shorter than the true hiking distances.

1. Select the ROUTE page on your receiver.

2. Select NEW or an unused route on the screen.

3. In the first waypoint position, enter the name of the starting way-point for the route.

4. Continue entering waypoints in subsequent positions in the order you want to go to them.

5. Name the route and save it in the memory.

Once a route has been entered and saved, you can use it for navigation. Again, check your instruction manual for details. Typically, you go to the ROUTE page, choose the route you want, and select the key labeled something like NAVIGATE, FOLLOW, or ACTIVATE.

The first waypoint in the route is always your starting point, not your first destination. So when you activate a route, it immediately directs you to the second waypoint, even if you are nowhere near the starting point. You might wonder why you even need to enter the starting point, but just remember it becomes very important if you plan to use the route reversal feature to lead you back to the beginning.

Planning a Route with Software Maps

Route planning with paper maps is tedious, especially when it comes to reading waypoint coordinates. Software maps make the process much easier. You can easily draw your intended route onto the map, read its total length, and generate an elevation profile. You can quickly place waypoints on the route and electronically transfer their coordinates to your GPS receiver. Once you have used software maps, you'll find it difficult to go back to using paper maps.

Let's take a quick look at how you would plan the same route to the top of Half Dome using a software map. This example will use National Geographic's Topo! State-Series software for California, but the process is similar for other software packages.

After installing the software on your PC, launch the program and zoom in on the area around Half Dome. With Topo!, the highest zoom level displays USGS 7.5-minute maps. The first difference you'll notice is its seamless coverage. You'll hardly even be aware that the trail stretches across two paper maps. Topo! also gives you the convenience of selecting coordinates in either latitude and longitude (in any of the three formats) or UTM, and selecting either the NAD 27 or WGS 84 datum. You access these choices from its PREFERENCES menu.

Next, use the "Route" tool to draw your intended trail on the display. (Note that although Topo! calls this a "route," it is actually a "track" or

Software maps make it easy to create waypoints and load them into your GPS receiver. This is the waypoint screen from National Geographic's Topo! software. (Map created with Topo! ©2006 National Geographic)

After creating a list of waypoints, it can easily be uploaded to a GPS receiver. (Map created with Topo! ©2006 National Geographic)

"trail" in GPS parlance.) It takes a little practice to draw an accurate trail using Topo!'s tool. You'll probably need to use the right mouse button to erase mistakes several times along the way. But with care, you'll eventually end up with a reasonable representation of the trail. When finished, click the left mouse button to end the trail. A dialogue box appears that shows the trail's total length, gives you the option of naming it, and allows you to do things like change the line style or build an elevation profile.

Now you're ready to create the GPS route by adding waypoints using the "Waypoint" tool. Click the pointer on each location where you want to add a waypoint and a dialogue box comes up giving you the location and other information. Highlight the name box and type in the new name. Click "OK," and the waypoint shows up on the screen. Do this for each waypoint you want to add. When finished, you'll have a list of waypoints ready to be loaded into your GPS receiver. Connect your receiver to your computer using the appropriate cable, and select the HANDHELDS menu to upload the information—much simpler and more foolproof than using paper maps.

Part III
Recovering from Disaster

Key Concepts

- ▶ **Essential items for wilderness travel**

- ▶ **Planning ahead to avoid disaster**

- ▶ **Basic map and compass skills**

- ▶ **Wilderness navigation without GPS**

- ▶ **Advantages of waiting for rescue versus finding your own way out**

- ▶ **Primitive methods for finding your way without a map or compass**

Preparing for Disaster

The chapters in this section deal with the inevitable question: "What do I do when I'm out in the wilderness and my GPS receiver fails?" First, let me point out that this is not a book on outdoor survival. If you intend to spend much time in the wilderness, you should know many survival techniques that aren't covered here. Check the references in Appendix II for information on wilderness survival. What this section will cover are alternate navigation techniques—methods you can use to get back to safety if you unexpectedly find yourself without a working GPS receiver.

Essential Items

The best way to deal with disaster is to avoid it in the first place. It doesn't take a lot of preparation to turn what could have been a serious incident into something that's little more than a momentary inconvenience. Many books provide lists of "10 Essentials" that should be carried by every outdoor adventurer. The first list was originally compiled by The Mountaineers back in the 1930s for use by climbers. Updated for today's needs, it is a good list for anyone intending to travel more than an hour or two from civilization. Everything here should fit in an ordinary daypack with room to spare:

1. **Extra clothing.** Even if you plan to go out for only a dayhike, take a few key items of clothing. You primarily need protection against unexpectedly cool and windy weather, and perhaps the occasional rain shower. Check the weather forecast for the next several days and pack the minimum you think you would need if you were stuck overnight. A windproof jacket is essential. Without a windproof shell, an ordinary fleece jacket won't protect you in even moderate winds. If rain is even remotely possible, your jacket should be waterproof. Be wary of inexpensive nylon clothing advertised as "water resistant." Such material isn't designed to keep you dry for extended periods. "Waterproof-breathable"

fabric is more expensive but well worth it if you're caught in a downpour.

Long pants and a wide-brimmed hat are also important. Cargo pants with zip-off legs let you easily adapt to changing weather conditions without adding much bulk in a daypack. Other recommended items are an extra pair of socks (in case you get wet crossing a stream), and gloves and a warm hat to help keep you warm if you get delayed overnight. Finally, you should always have an aluminum-coated Mylar "space blanket" stowed for an emergency. It weighs next to nothing and can keep you remarkably warm if necessary.

2.   **Extra food and water.** You don't need to pack four-course meals if you're only planning to be out for the morning, but you should always have extra rations to tide you over in an emergency. Energy bars, beef jerky, and freeze-dried backpacker meals (if you have water and a way to heat them) are good alternatives. These rations should be in addition to the food you already planned to bring. Plan so that if nothing goes wrong, you'll still have food left at the end of your journey.

Carry plenty of water, even in regions where ground water is readily available. These days, you need to purify water from almost all natural sources, so you might want to carry water-purification tablets or a water filter as well. When purchasing a filter, look for one rated to 0.2 micron, which will not only screen out giardia, the most common problem, but also other harmful bacteria. Note that water filters won't kill viruses unless they also include an iodine treatment—not usually a problem in the US but a definite concern in the third world. Water-purification tablets do kill viruses but leave a distinctive chemical taste. Tablets don't have an indefinite shelf life and deteriorate quickly after the bottle is opened. Follow the instructions on the bottle to understand proper use.

3.   **Sunglasses.** When this list was originally developed in the 1930s, sunglasses were a relative rarity. Now they are routine. Admittedly, they aren't essential in every case, but research has shown that excessive exposure to the sun is associated with eye cataracts and macular degeneration. If you expect to travel over sand, snow, or water, they are required to prevent temporary or permanent eye damage from reflected sunlight. Make sure they are rated to block 100 percent of both UVA and UVB rays.

4. **Knife/multipurpose tool.** The Swiss Army knife has been the tried-and-true staple for many years. It's still a good choice, but these days many people have come to prefer a multipurpose tool that includes pliers, scissors, screwdrivers, and numerous other implements in addition to the basic knife. Models by Leatherman (www.leatherman.com) and Gerber (www.gerbertools.com) are well-designed, reliable, and priced to match.

5. **Matches and fire starter.** Although you may take a good supply of ordinary matches, make sure you supplement those with specialty waterproof matches. You might also consider packing a butane pocket lighter. Everyone in your group except small children should carry his or her own supply of matches.

    Even in wooded areas, it might not be that easy to start a fire in an emergency. You don't want to waste all your matches trying to light damp leaves or green pine needles. Solid-fuel tablets or jellied-fuel tubes, available at camping supply stores, can get a roaring fire started with just one match. Even a simple candle can be better than nothing.

6. **Whistle/signaling device.** A simple whistle kept in a pocket or lashed to a backpack works much better than your lungs at calling for help—especially for children, whose voices don't carry very far. The universal signal for help is three short blasts repeated at regular intervals.

7. **First-aid kit.** At minimum, a first-aid kit should include gloves, adhesive bandages, a few larger gauze pads, aspirin or ibuprofen, adhesive tape, antibacterial ointment, a good pair of tweezers, and a first-aid instruction manual. For larger groups or extended trips, the kit should necessarily be larger and more extensive. One generally useful item is a 25-foot length of braided nylon or parachute cord. Check your local outdoor specialty shop for pre-assembled kits, or study their contents to aid in assembling your own.

8. **Flashlight.** As with matches, everyone in a group should carry at least a small flashlight. Those by Mag-Lite (www.maglite.com) are durable and reliable. You may also want to check out some of the newer LED-based flashlights that put out bright illumination with less drain on batteries than incandescent lights. Headlamps also have become popular, as they allow you to keep both hands free for other activities.

9/10. **Map and compass.** As already described, a map and compass are essential any time you venture into the wilderness. You'll also want a pen or pencil to make notations on the map.

Of course, if you only intend to travel through the local park, a survival kit this extensive is hardly necessary. But the subject of this section is recovering from disaster; if you drop and break your GPS receiver in the local park, it might be a disaster to your pocketbook but hardly something that will keep you from finding your way home. For the kinds of wilderness travels implied in these chapters, every one of these essentials should be in your pack.

GPS Survival Kit

The GPS navigator needs to expand on this list slightly by adding three additional things:

▶ GPS receiver

▶ Sturdy carrying case

▶ Extra batteries

Remember: Your GPS receiver does not replace the map and compass, it is in addition to them. You still need the map and compass so you can navigate if your GPS receiver fails. In the next chapter, you'll see how to do this.

It's important to keep your receiver in a carrying case when it is not being used. A GPS receiver is not indestructible, and letting it bang around loosely in your pack or pocket will only hasten its demise. On some receivers, the connections between the LCD display and the internal electronics are particularly susceptible. If you start noticing lines running horizontally or vertically through the display, you'll know the connections are suspect. Sometimes you can temporarily solve the problem by striking the receiver against the palm of your hand (never anything harder), but only try this as a last resort.

The carrying case can be one originally designed for a digital camera or one that has been custom-designed for your receiver. The important thing is that it be sufficiently padded to provide reasonable protection.

Extra batteries are an absolute necessity. Stick a few extra AA cells (or whatever your receiver requires) in your pocket or backpack, or in the side pocket of your receiver's case, if it has one. You'll have cheap, lightweight insurance against unexpected power loss. Not having spare batteries in the wilderness should be a criminal offense.

These backup batteries should be alkaline, not NiCad or NiMH rechargeables. Alkalines will not only keep your receiver operating longer (more than twice as many hours as NiCad), they also have a considerably longer shelf life. NiCad and NiMH rechargeables will slowly discharge just sitting on the shelf, and after only a few weeks, they will need to be recharged. Rechargeable batteries are fine for casual use on dayhikes where you have easy access to a charger, but don't rely on them in the wilderness. For cold-weather use, you might even want to consider lithium batteries. Although they're much more expensive than alkalines, their cold-weather performance is considerably better. See page 192 or check your GPS receiver's instruction manual for more information on battery compatibility.

Other Backup Plans

The more care you put into planning your adventure ahead of time, the less likely you are to get into serious trouble. In addition to the 10 essentials, here are a few other things you can do to reduce the risk of disaster.

Spare GPS receiver. Aircraft, ships, and spacecraft all have double or triple redundant navigation systems. When your life depends on it, you can't allow yourself to be put in jeopardy by a single instrument failure. The serious outdoor navigator would do well to consider the same possibility and invest in a second GPS receiver as a backup.

This recommendation isn't intended to stimulate the economy by helping sell GPS receivers. If your safety doesn't depend on your GPS receiver, if you can find your way home without it, you probably don't need to make the investment. But if you plan a journey into serious wilderness—the wilds of Alaska or the Australian Outback, for example—ask yourself just how important it is that you have a working GPS receiver. Spending an extra $100 on a backup receiver may be a minor additional expense compared to the total cost of your trip.

Lightweight models such as the Garmin Geko make it difficult to claim you can't afford the extra weight. Just be sure that if you bring a second receiver, you know how to use it. You don't want to be struggling to learn a new receiver at what is already a time of serious stress. This is one argument in favor of selecting a backup receiver from the same family as your primary receiver. It might not have all the same features, but at least it will have a familiar interface.

There are a couple of other things to remember when bringing a backup receiver. First, make sure it, too, has fresh batteries, and that you have appropriate spares. The Geko, for example, uses AAA batteries. Your primary receiver probably uses AA cells. So you would need to bring some of each.

Second, remember to turn on your backup receiver and mark your position at the beginning of the journey. It's best if you enter all the intermediate waypoints as well. If you get into a situation where you need to depend on a backup receiver to aid your return, you want to make sure it knows where you're going.

If there is more than one person in your party, spread the GPS receivers out among them. That way, if you get separated or someone loses a backpack over a cliff or down a river, you haven't also automatically lost your backup.

Cell phone. Another survival item you might be considering is a cellular telephone. In movies and television ads, such phones always work with crystal clarity. In the wilderness, though, they probably won't. Telephone companies are understandably driven by profit, so they install base stations in locations they know will get used. Wilderness areas aren't at the top of their coverage list.

Unless you know you are going to be within range of a cellular base station, you shouldn't depend on a cell phone to get you out of a fix. You might still want to bring it along, and you may be pleasantly surprised. In the California desert, I've gotten good reception 50 miles from the nearest habitation and well away from the coverage limits shown on the telephone company's maps. But I always regard such a result as a lucky happenstance and would never trust my safety to achieving a repeat performance.

Share your itinerary. Finally, any time you plan a journey into the wilderness, even if just for a few hours, you should let someone know your plan and when you intend to return. You never know when an accident might interrupt your travel. If you suddenly find yourself with a serious injury, you might not be able to get back, even if your GPS receiver is still working. If you don't return in a timely manner, there will at least be someone who can initiate a search-and-rescue operation.

Map and Compass Navigation

So far, maps and compasses have played only supporting roles in outdoor navigation. As long as you have a working GPS receiver with all necessary waypoints stored properly, you can safely use it as your primary navigation tool. But what do you do if your receiver fails? Perhaps the batteries died and you don't have spares. Or maybe it took a hard blow in a fall, breaking the display. Or even worse, maybe you lost it in a lake or over a precipitous chasm. Now what? How do you get back to safety?

This chapter assumes you've done the sensible thing and brought along a topo map and compass. It also assumes it's not as simple as following a well-marked trail back to your starting point. Perhaps it's been snowing and your tracks are covered. Maybe you've done serious cross-country hiking or spent the day canoeing on a remote, unfamiliar lake. You need to get back using only your map, compass, and navigation skills. This chapter won't teach you everything about map and compass navigation, but you'll learn enough to get by in an emergency.

First, remember to stay calm. You've sensibly packed a map and compass, so you're already halfway home. Now you just need to relax and remember how to use them. With a map and compass, getting back to safety involves four steps:

1. Determine your present position.
2. Decide on your destination.
3. Identify the best route to get there.
4. Follow the chosen route, making adjustments as necessary along the way.

Determining Your Present Position

Before you can figure out how to get to safety, you first have to know where you are. Don't panic and start heading in a random direction or in what you think might be the right direction without confirming it. Take the time to really identify where you are.

One fundamental skill you should make a habit is to regularly correlate your GPS position with the map. That way, if the receiver fails, you already have a good idea of your location. Unfortunately, too many people fail to do this. How do you find your position when you haven't been keeping careful track? This section describes three ways: triangulation, dead reckoning, and altimeter navigation. But none of these is as good as correlating your position as you travel.

Triangulation

The easiest approach, if the opportunity presents itself, is to triangulate your position from objects you can see in the landscape. It's similar to how your GPS receiver works, but of course you're not using satellites, so you must use identifiable objects in the landscape.

Orienting the map. You first need to orient your map to the surroundings. When you're facing north, you want the top of the map to also be facing north. That way, it's easy to match a feature in the distance to its corresponding feature on the map.

Do this by using your compass. Set it to an indicated true bearing of 0° and lay the compass pointing north on the map so the side of the compass aligns with a map border (neatline) as shown in the photo.

To orient your map to the surroundings, set the bearing indicator to 0° true and align the edge of the compass with the neatline of the map. Rotate map and compass together to box the magnetic needle inside the north reference indicator. Note this compass has been adjusted to compensate for magnetic declination.

Now rotate your map and compass together until the magnetic needle is boxed inside the north reference indicator. Your map is now aligned to the landscape.

This only works with a compass that's been set to compensate for local declination. Otherwise, you need to make the adjustment by mentally correcting for declination—not something you will want to worry about when you're already stressed from having just lost your primary navigation tool. This is where you will really appreciate a compass with adjustable declination. Now would be a good time to brush up on the principles of declination correction described on pages 44 and 45.

Triangulating your position. Now that you've got the map properly oriented, you're ready to triangulate your position. Here's how:

1. Identify at least two objects (preferably three) in your field of view that are also on the map. These can be prominent mountain peaks, radio towers, waterfalls, or just about anything else you can reliably identify in both your surroundings and on the map. Ideally, the objects should be at close to right angles from each other, though this is not always possible. Avoid objects that are in line or 180° apart.

   If you happen to be on a known river, trail, ridge line, gully, or similar geographic feature, you only need to identify one additional object (preferably two). Such features are known as handrails, and you can use them to help identify your position.

   If you can't spot suitable objects from your current position, do a little reconnaissance. Climb to the top of a nearby hill (if you can do it safely) or move to an area with a better view—a meadow or forest clearing, for example. Be cautious when moving, and don't lose visual contact with others in your party.

2. Use your compass to read the bearing to each object. (If you need a refresher on taking a bearing, refer to page 47.) You will be plotting these bearings on the map, so they need to be referenced to true north. Again, I'll recommend you invest in a compass with adjustable declination and get comfortable using it.

   Take care to get your compass readings as accurate as possible. It's a little easier with a mirror compass, as you can view both the object and the compass vial at the same time. With a simple baseplate compass, you'll have to point it carefully at the object before rotating the vial. Be sure to keep the compass level so the magnetic needle rotates freely.

   As shown in the diagram on page 110, the uncertainty in your position increases the farther you are from the reference object. If

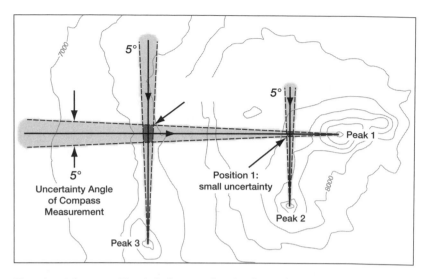

When triangulating your position, the farther you are from the reference object, the greater the uncertainty in your position. This example assumes you can measure an object's bearing to an accuracy of 5 degrees. At Position 1, you are close to the reference objects, and the uncertainty is small. At Position 2, the uncertainty is larger, especially because you are far from Peak 1.

you can only measure an object's bearing to within 5 degrees, the uncertainty in your position will be 450 feet per mile. If the object is a mountain peak 10 miles away, your uncertainty is 4500 feet—nearly a mile. By improving the accuracy of your measurements to 2 degrees, the uncertainty drops to only 180 feet per mile—a good reason to measure bearings as accurately as possible.

With two people, you can improve the accuracy of measurements taken with a simple baseplate compass. One person kneels down, holds the compass at eye level (keeping it level), and points it at the object. The other person remains standing to view the compass vial. This person carefully rotates the vial to center the compass needle inside the north reference indicator while the kneeling person keeps the compass level and pointed at the object.

3. Correct the measured bearings for magnetic declination, if necessary.

4. For each object, draw a line on the map through the object at the bearing angle you measured to it. This line is known as a position line. You know that you must be somewhere along this line.

In this situation, the bearings you measured are from your unknown position to the known object. This is opposite of the situation described in Chapter 3, where you knew your current position but

To triangulate your position, plot the bearings you have measured from your current position to at least two (preferably three) objects you have identified on the map. Notice that with three objects, the lines probably won't all intersect at the same spot. You are most likely somewhere within the triangle of uncertainty.

not your destination. In this case, after setting the correct bearing on the vial, lay the compass on the map so the direction-of-travel arrow points in the direction of the object. The front edge of the compass should be touching it, as shown in the illustration. Now adjust the entire compass (don't turn the vial!) so that 0° points to the top of the map, while the front edge of the compass remains in contact with the object. (Don't worry about where the magnetic needle points.) Some compasses include north-south orienting lines to make this job a little easier.

Using a pencil, draw a line along the edge of the compass from the known object toward your location. If the distance is farther than the length of the compass, use a straightedge to extend it. In the unlikely event that you've brought along a ruler for this purpose, that's great. Otherwise, find something else long and straight—the edge of a book or map, for instance. You can also make your own straightedge by folding a sheet of paper in half or tightly stretching a piece of string or fishing line.

5. If you took bearings to two or more objects, your position is where the lines intersect. If you took only one bearing and used a known feature like a river as a handrail, your position is where the bearing line intersects the handrail.

Triangulation is a reasonably accurate way to find your position, though it's not perfect. You'll quickly discover this if you take bearings to more than two objects and plot all the position lines on the map. It's unlikely they'll all intersect at the same spot, but if you've made careful measurements, they should be close. The distance between the various intersections is a good approximation of the error in your measurements.

To read the bearing of an object with a mirror compass, aim the notch on top of the lid at the object so the line down the center of the mirror runs through the apparent center of the vial. Rotate the vial while watching it in the mirror until the north reference indicator aligns with the magnetic needle.

Dead Reckoning

Suppose you can't spot any identifiable features in the landscape—there's nothing but forest or unbroken swampland, for instance, or perhaps it's foggy. Now it becomes more of a challenge. Your objective becomes one of navigating in the correct general direction until you can get to a more identifiable area. This is known by mariners as dead reckoning (where "dead" doesn't necessarily reflect on the fate of its user, but rather is short for "deduced").

Here is where you need to stop and think. You should know where on the map you started from, and you will usually have a general idea of what direction you have been traveling. You should also have some idea of how long you have been out. If you can estimate how far you have traveled and what direction you have been moving, you can get a rough idea of where you are from your starting point.

Estimating the distance traveled. Your first task is to estimate the distance you have traveled. If you have been hiking, you can apply some general guidelines (for other modes of transportation you'll have to make your own estimates). I'll caution you that it's always risky to publish such guidelines, because every situation is different. A young athlete with only a water bottle will move significantly faster than a 50-year-old office manager carrying a 40-pound pack.

With that caution in mind, here is a very simplified, two-step approach: You first need to estimate your average speed. Then you need to estimate how long you have been traveling. Knowing these two things, you can estimate distance you have covered.

In this simplified approach, assume you can travel at a standard speed on level ground. Then adjust that rate to account for terrain that requires climbing or descending, and make a further adjustment to account for the type of terrain. This simplified approach does not take into account fatigue.

The following guidelines provide a starting point for estimating walking speeds. (Don't hesitate to modify the numbers to account for your own hiking style.)

▶ On level ground and average terrain, figure you can walk about 2 miles per hour when carrying a moderate pack up to about 30 pounds.

▶ For every 200 feet per mile of elevation gain, deduct 0.3 mile per hour.

▶ For every 200 feet per mile of elevation drop, deduct 0.1 mile per hour.

▶ When walking over soft sand or loose rock, cut the calculated speed in half.

These guidelines apply for elevation gains or losses up to about 800 feet per mile (17 percent grade). Beyond that, you're on your own.

Let's look at an example: Suppose you are hiking a trail that climbs 400 feet in 1 mile. Your approximate speed is therefore 2 miles per hour, minus 0.3 × 2, or 1.4 miles per hour. If your journey was over soft sand, cut the number in half, to 0.7 mile per hour. Of course, these are only generalizations; your mileage may vary. You should do a few hikes in controlled conditions to calibrate your normal speed.

Estimating elevation change. You now know how to estimate your speed, but how do you determine the amount of elevation gain or loss? The easiest way is to use your topo map and a piece of string. You first need to calibrate the string using the scale at the bottom of the map. Stretch the string between your thumbs so they are exactly a scale mile apart. Then, holding the string tightly, arrange it so it aligns with your approximate route. Read the elevation contours at your starting and ending points. The difference is the elevation gain or loss in 1 mile. If you've traveled more than a mile, divide the total elevation change by the total distance, or take several 1-mile-long readings along your path and use the average.

Estimating your location. Now you have an estimate of your speed and how long you have been hiking. Multiply your speed by your travel time to get the distance traveled. Here's an example: You've been out for six

To determine the change in elevation per mile, calculate the total elevation change and divide by the total distance traveled. You can measure distance by laying a string along your approximate path, then calibrating it against the map scale. A knot at one end of the string makes the measurement easier. In this example, the total elevation change is 800 feet, and the total distance is 1.5 miles, so the climb is about 500 feet per mile.

hours. You estimate you've been climbing at a rate of 400 feet per mile over average terrain, so your hiking speed has been 1.4 miles per hour. Multiply 1.4 miles per hour by six hours to get a total distance of 8.4 miles. You'd probably want to reduce that a bit to account for fatigue and the occasional rest stop you took along the way.

Finally, draw a line on the map from your starting point in the general direction you estimate you've been heading. You are most likely somewhere along this line. If you had been hiking in a straight line the entire time, you would be about 7 to 8 miles away, but that's not usually the case. Here is where you have to apply some judgment and estimate how your actual course came into play. Again, you can use a string that you've calibrated to be about 8 scale miles long. Arrange it in what you believe to be roughly approximate your true course to get an idea of where you are.

Altimeter Navigation

Before the advent of GPS, navigation by barometric altimeter was a fairly well-known, though infrequently used, backup method. These days, you don't hear too much about it. But you can still use it to advantage—if you remembered to pack a barometric altimeter. I'm not talking about the one you might have in your fancy, high-end GPS receiver. If its batteries have run down or you've lost it over a cliff, its internal altimeter will be no more useful to you than its GPS functions. For this approach to work, you need a separate, backup altimeter.

Altimeters come in two varieties: mechanical units with analog dials and electronic units with digital displays. Thommen (www.thommen. aero) is an example of a manufacturer of precision analog altimeters. Brunton (www.brunton.com) makes a fine digital unit, the ADC Summit, which also doubles as a wind-speed indicator and thermometer. You can also find reasonably good digital altimeters on some high-end watches designed for outdoor adventurers. Digital units usually provide higher-resolution readouts, often calibrated to display differences of only a few feet. Analog units generally are calibrated in 20- to 100-foot increments, although you can do a pretty good job of eyeballing intermediate values. Remember, there is a difference between readout resolution and true accuracy. Given that you won't usually be able to calibrate your altimeter to better than 20-foot accuracy anyway, the resolution of a good mechanical unit is more than adequate.

Before you start using a barometric altimeter, you need to understand a little about how it works. As its name implies, it doesn't directly measure true elevation, but rather barometric pressure. Since barometric pressure decreases in a predictable way as you gain elevation, it is possible for the altimeter to give a readout of elevation.

As is usually the case with such matters, it isn't as simple as it first sounds. Barometric pressure is not constant, but changes depending on the weather, which is why a barometer is useful as a weather forecasting tool. Before you can take accurate elevation readings, you first have to perform a calibration. You do this by going to a known elevation and adjusting your altimeter to read that elevation. This can be a trailhead, visitors center, or any other location where the elevation is either posted or can be determined from your topo map. The closer you are to the elevations

The Thommen Classic is an example of a precision mechanical altimeter. (Courtesy of Revue Thommen AG)

you plan to hike, the better. Avoid calibrating your altimeter at sea level when you plan to be hiking at 8000 feet.

Over the course of a day, barometric pressure will change with the weather, causing your apparent elevation to change even if you are standing still. But the effect is less than you might think. If the weather is changing, you may see your apparent elevation change by as much as 100 feet over the course of a few hours. Usually, the change is much less. Changes in temperature can also introduce large errors, particularly with an inexpensive altimeter that doesn't include some sort of temperature compensator. Even if it does, it's never a good idea to keep your altimeter in a warm vest pocket, then take it out and try to make an accurate elevation reading in near freezing temperatures.

You can help compensate for these errors by periodically recalibrating over the course of the day when you reach points of known elevation. These don't need to be places where thoughtful rangers have posted elevation signs. As you hike, look for points you can identify on the map: things like trail junctions or locations where a stream intersects the trail, for example. Then check your topo map. You can get a pretty good idea of your elevation by studying the contour lines around your known location. If your altimeter no longer matches, reset it.

In general, you shouldn't use the elevation readout from your GPS receiver to calibrate a barometric altimeter. GPS elevations are significantly less accurate than GPS horizontal positions. You're better off calibrating your altimeter from your topo map.

Now that you know how to calibrate an altimeter, let's see how to use it in navigation. Basically, knowing your elevation gives you a handrail with which to work. On the topo map, you know you are somewhere along a line representing your measured elevation. If you can find the bearing to just one object on the map, your location will be the intersection of that bearing with the line of known elevation.

Refer to the illustration on page 117 for an example. Suppose you have been cross-country hiking in the area around Freezeout Creek when the batteries in your GPS receiver fail. As you look around, you can see only one recognizable feature, a radio tower toward the northeast. Thankfully, you brought along your altimeter and remembered to calibrate it before you left. You take a reading and find your elevation is 800 feet. Next, you take a compass bearing to the radio tower and find it is at a true bearing of 75 degrees (remember to correct for declination if you haven't adjusted your compass for the local declination).

Pull out your topo map, find the radio tower, and use your compass to plot a bearing line through it at 75 degrees. Remember that this is the bearing from your current position to the radio tower, so you have to be somewhere to the southwest, along the elevation contour of 800 feet.

When you know your elevation and the bearing to an object in the distance, your position is at the intersection of the bearing line and your elevation.

Notice that the 800-foot contour line intersects the bearing line on either side of Freezeout Creek—once on the downslope and once on the upslope. With a little thought, you realize your immediate terrain slopes downward in the direction of the tower, so you must be at the more westerly intersection.

Identifying Your Destination

Now that you know where you are, you're well on your way to getting back. Remember once again the Cardinal Rule of GPS Navigation introduced in Chapter 1: *It doesn't do you any good to know where you are if you don't know where you want to go.* Even without a working GPS receiver, that's important to remember. Now it's time to figure out your destination.

Often this will be easy. You want to get back to where you started. But this might not always be the best choice. It might be getting dark, or you might be injured, and you just want to find the quickest way to civilization. Check the map for promising nearby features. You may be much closer to a paved highway than to your vehicle parked along a lonely Forest Service road. If there's little hope of getting out today, look for a likely spot to spend the night: a ski hut, abandoned ranch house, or perhaps a sheltered cove with a natural spring you can use for drinking water.

Once you've decided on your destination, mark it on the map with a big "X." That way, in the heat of the moment, you're less likely to get confused and start heading toward the wrong objective.

Planning the Route

Now it's time to plan the route to your destination. Even if you intend to go back where you started, you might not want to travel the same route you took out. With a working GPS receiver, you really didn't have to worry about the exact route to a destination; your receiver was always updating your bearing. Now, with just a map and compass, you probably want to simplify things.

Unless you're really close to your destination, you probably won't be able to get to it in a straight shot. Just as you use GPS waypoints to create multileg routes, you'll probably need to identify several intermediate destinations. These could be things like stream crossings, ridge lines, trails, or artificial features like radio towers. Make sure these are features you can readily identify when you arrive at them. You don't want to compound your problems by blindly hiking past your goal because you didn't recognize it when you got there.

At this point, you have identified where you are, where you want to go, and the intermediate points along the way. You have one more thing to do before you begin hiking: You need to measure the compass bearing and estimate the distance from each intermediate destination to the next.

This is the same process as described more thoroughly in Chapter 3. Start with the bearing from your present position to your first intermediate goal. Lay the compass on the map with its direction-of-travel arrow pointing toward the first goal, then rotate the compass vial so that 0° points straight up (don't worry about where the magnetic needle points). Use the vial's north-south orienting lines, if it has them, as alignment aids. Then read the bearing as the number where the vial meets the bearing indicator. Now estimate the distance between points using the map scale and a piece of string. Write the bearing and distance on the map so you don't forget it. Repeat the process for each intermediate leg. Once you've done this, you're ready to roll.

Following the Route

The first thing to do is go back and read the section on following a bearing, on page 48 in Chapter 3. Many of the same principles apply here.

Foremost is the caution against blindly trying to follow a straight-line route to your destination. Also remember the concept of navigating by visible reference points you've selected in the distance. Don't forget to triangulate your position occasionally as you travel, and update it on the map. And use the methods for estimating travel time on pages 112 and 113 to help determine when you should be approaching a destination.

Although there are many similarities, navigating a route by map and compass alone is a little different than using a GPS receiver. With GPS, you aren't so concerned about following a precise path because your receiver is constantly updating your bearing. With only a map and compass, you're not so fortunate. Once you unknowingly get off track, there is no easy way to self-correct. And you will get off track; in the wilderness, it isn't easy to navigate a precise bearing over any appreciable distance.

Aiming Off

Experienced navigators compensate for this by a technique known as "aiming off." The concept is really quite simple. Let's say your objective is the one passable crossing of an otherwise dangerous river. From the map, you see the bearing to this crossing is 115 degrees. If you try to follow that exact bearing, you will inevitably miss your objective, but you won't know which direction you are off. When you reach the river, do you turn right or left to find the crossing?

The question is more easily answered if you deliberately navigated slightly off course, say, to the left of the true bearing. When you reach the river, you might not know exactly how far it is to the crossing, but at least you'll know you need to turn right. How much should you aim off? There's no standard answer, but 10 degrees left or 10 degrees right is a

Concept of aiming off

good starting point. Decide whether to navigate right or left after study-ing the map to see which direction has the less hostile terrain.

Aiming off doesn't work so well if your destination isn't located along a suitable handrail like a river or trail. With a calibrated altimeter, you can still attempt the technique by using elevation as a handrail, but remember that you can probably only determine your elevation to an accuracy of 40 or 50 feet. In this case, you will want a destination that is readily visible, even when you can only get within the general area.

Navigating Around Obstacles

Another thing you'll want to know is how to navigate around un-foreseen obstacles. Even a 7.5-minute USGS quad with a 40-foot contour interval won't show you every potential obstacle. A ridge that looked inconsequential on the map might be insurmountable in real life. Or a normally placid creek might be swollen from recent rains. Either way, you need to take a detour, then get back on course.

Here's how to do it: When you come to an obstacle, determine the angle necessary to deviate around it. Navigate this new bearing for a spe-cific amount of time, then reverse your bearing for the same amount of time. If you've done everything right, you will be back on your original course and can return to your original bearing.

Let's look at an example: Suppose you are following a bearing of 100 degrees when you hit an ephemeral lake created by melting spring snow. You have no choice; you have to go around it. After studying the terrain, you decide to alter your course 45 degrees to the left. Your new

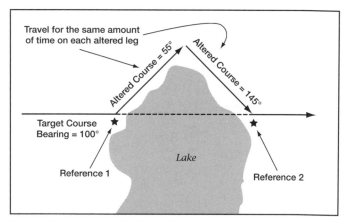

Concept of navigating around an obstacle. To improve accuracy, identify landmarks at both near and far sides of the lake to use as references. When you reach the far side, sight from 2 back to 1 to confirm you are again on track.

bearing is then 100 degrees minus 45 degrees, or 55 degrees. Set this bearing on your compass and hike until you are sure you are past the apex of the obstacle. Keep careful track of how long you are traveling on this course deviation.

To determine the bearing necessary to get back to your original course, calculate the complementary bearing: 100 degrees plus 45 degrees, or 145 degrees. Assuming you're on similar terrain, hike this bearing for the same amount of time, and you should be back in line with your original track. If the terrain is substantially different—say, one leg is downhill and the other is uphill—use the method for estimating travel speed described earlier in this chapter to determine when you have covered the equivalent distance. You can now set your compass back to 100 degrees and continue on course.

A second example will illustrate another thing to consider about compass bearings: how to deal with math that crosses through a bearing of 0 degrees or 360 degrees. Suppose you are navigating a bearing of 40 degrees when you come to a swollen river perpendicular to your path. You know your best bet for a safe crossing is to your left, so you need to adjust your compass bearing left by 90 degrees. Your new bearing is 40 degrees minus 90 degrees, or -50 degrees. Search as you might, you won't find a bearing of *negative* 50 degrees anywhere on your compass. Whenever you end up with a negative bearing, you must subtract that number from 360 degrees. In this case, your bearing is 360 degrees minus 50 degrees, or 310 degrees.

Similarly, if you were hiking a bearing of 310 degrees and needed to turn 90 degrees to the right, your calculated bearing would be 310 degrees plus 90 degrees, or 400 degrees. Whenever this number is larger than 360 degrees, you must subtract 360 degrees from it. So your new bearing would be 400 degrees minus 360 degrees, or 40 degrees.

There are many other tricks of the trade used by skilled map-and-compass navigators, but these are beyond the scope of this book. If you really want to learn more, check out the sources listed in Appendix II. But if not, don't worry. The concepts covered in this chapter should be enough to get you out of difficulty when your GPS receiver fails. Just remember, they won't work if you haven't bothered to pack a map and compass.

Primitive
Navigation Techniques

Even if you're diligent about preparing for disaster, there may come a time when you face a more difficult situation. You're deep in the wilderness, your GPS receiver is lost or broken, and you don't have a map or a compass. Perhaps a bag got lost overboard on a canoe trip, or you've been separated from a companion who had all the navigation gear. Now what do you do?

The first thing to do is to sit down and catch your breath. Don't let panic set in. Remember that generations of adventurers—Daniel Boone, Davy Crockett, and countless other mountain men—regularly traveled through virgin wilderness without so much as map and compass, let alone a GPS receiver. If they could do it, there's hope for you.

You first have to decide whether it's more sensible to try to find your way out, or whether you should just sit and wait for a rescue party. If you've been separated from a group or if you told someone of your plans and your expected return, you will probably be better off sitting and waiting, especially if you're injured or disoriented. Rescue teams lament the all-too-frequent story of a lost hiker continuing to wander like a moving target, almost as if he were deliberately avoiding rescue. Search efforts are conducted in a planned way, so if the hiker wanders from an area that hasn't been searched into one that already has, his chances of being found alive diminish considerably.

Once you have decided to wait, there are a few things to keep in mind that will aid your rescue. Rather than continuing to wander, put your energy into two efforts: finding suitable shelter and making yourself obvious to the search team. That way, you're more likely to still be alive when you're eventually found.

Plan for the night well in advance. If the weather is bad, seek shelter under trees or rock alcoves. If you've got matches (you should always carry waterproof matches in the wilderness), start a signal fire. Even if people aren't yet looking for you, billowing smoke in a wilderness area may be spotted by a fire lookout or reported to authorities by others in the area. The fire's heat will also keep you warm during the long night. Just be careful about keeping the fire under control, or you could suddenly find yourself in an even worse situation.

Self-Rescue

If you know a search team won't be dispatched, or if your party includes a seriously injured member who needs urgent attention, you may decide it's better to find your own way out. Without map or compass, the task is more challenging, but not impossible. As you learned in the last chapter, there are four steps to the process: determining where you are, deciding where you want to go, picking the route, and following it to your destination.

At this point, most books tell you how to figure out where north is when you don't have a compass. I'll do that in a moment. But finding north solves only part of the problem. Similar to the Cardinal Rule of GPS Navigation, there is what I call a more general Cardinal Rule of Navigation:

It doesn't do you any good to know which direction is north if you don't know which direction you want to travel.

So before you spend time finding north, ask and answer these three questions:

1. Where am I?
2. Where do I want to go?
3. What direction do I need to go to get there?

Answering the first question may seem impossible. Your initial reaction might be, "If I knew where I was, I wouldn't be lost." But with a little thought, you should be able to come up with at least a general idea.

There may be times when it doesn't really matter. Hike for a few hours in any direction, and you're sure to hit some sort of civilization. If so, that's great. You don't need to know the techniques described here. But sometimes you will be in a situation in which hiking in most directions will only carry you deeper into the wilderness. There might only be one direction that gets you back to civilization, and that's the one you need to follow.

If you really have no idea where you are and have decided to find your own way out rather than wait for rescue, one approach is to follow a stream or river in the direction it flows. It should eventually reach a larger river or lake, where you have a better chance of finding civilization.

Another alternative is to scan the night sky for the telltale glow of habitation. But make sure you aren't fooled by a rising or setting moon. Mark the direction on the ground and wait for morning when it is safe to travel. (Night travel is generally not advised except in desert regions when the heat of the day makes travel impractical.)

If these approaches don't work, you'll need to gather your thoughts and list what you do know. The situation is similar to the discussion of dead reckoning in Chapter 9. All you may believe is that you've generally hiked in a northwesterly direction for about seven hours, but even that's enough to get started. At least you then know that hiking southeast for a similar amount of time should get you in the vicinity of your starting point.

The techniques described here show you ways to roughly identify a specific direction, not just north. Some methods give you south, east, or west. Those probably won't be any of the directions you want to head, but once you know a specific direction, you can sketch out a compass rose like the one shown on page 34 in Chapter 3 to find the direction you want to travel.

A couple of words of caution: These methods work in the temperate latitudes of the northern hemisphere. Methods for finding direction in the tropics or southern hemisphere are beyond the scope of this book. Also be aware that none of these techniques gives you the ability to navigate with pinpoint accuracy. But they might at least get you within earshot of a road or visual range of a small town.

Celestial Navigation Techniques

Celestial navigation has been practiced for centuries by mariners sailing the world's oceans. Some of their tried-and-true methods are easily adapted for emergency use on land. These are the methods that don't require the use of elaborate tables or complicated mathematics, neither of which is likely to be practical if you're lost in the wilderness.

Polaris. By far the most accurate method of finding direction without a compass is to use the stars. In Mexico, the US, and more northerly latitudes, the North Star, Polaris, is the easiest to identify. Polaris lies almost exactly due north, so close you can use it to determine magnetic declination. The easiest way to find Polaris is to first identify the Big Dipper. As shown in the diagram on page 126, the top of the Dipper points almost directly to Polaris.

In the late fall and early winter, the Big Dipper is low or even below the northern horizon in the evening, making it difficult or impossible to spot. At this time of year, the constellation Cassiopeia, looking

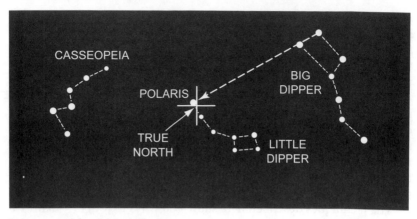

Finding true north from Polaris, the North Star

something like an upside-down "W," is a better reference. The top of the "W" points in the general direction of Polaris.

Orion. Another constellation many people can identify is Orion. The three stars of Orion's belt comprise one of the night sky's most notable features. Orion lies along the celestial equator, so no matter where you are, it essentially rises due east and sets due west. If you have a reasonable view of the horizon, you can see where it rises or sets and deduce the appropriate direction.

From about August through December, it's easiest to watch Orion as it rises in the east. In August, it rises in the early morning, between about 3 a.m. and 5 a.m., depending on your location. In December, it rises between 6 p.m. and 8 p.m. From late winter through late spring, it's easier to watch it setting in the west. The middle of summer is problematic because it rises after sunrise and sets before sunset. At that time of the year, you would need to use other stars along the celestial equator as your reference, but that's a subject beyond the scope of this book.

The main problem with celestial navigation on land is that your references are only visible at night. You don't want to be tramping through unknown wilderness in the dark, so the best thing to do is mark the measured direction on the ground in some way—a line in the dirt or a series of rocks, for example. Then wait until morning to start moving.

Directions from the Sun

There are several approaches to measuring direction from the sun, some reasonably accurate and others not. Here are three techniques, in rough order of accuracy.

Sun's Bearing at Noon

This approach can be quite accurate, if performed carefully. The principle is simple: By definition, the sun faces directly south at local noon. With the advent of accurate, quartz crystal-controlled watches, it's relatively easy to determine when it's noon. South is simply the direction to the sun at that instant.

The apparent position of the sun changes most rapidly in the hours around noon, so if you want to be accurate, you need to determine precisely when local noon occurs. The sun moves through an arc of 15 degrees every hour, or 1 degree for every four minutes of time. To find south to within 2 degrees, you need to take the reading within eight minutes of local noon.

During the months of daylight savings time, the largest potential source of error is forgetting to account for the time change. To figure out how to make the adjustment, remember the old saying, "spring forward, fall back." During daylight savings, clocks are moved forward one hour, so when the clock reads noon, it's really only 11 a.m. standard time. At this time of year, you need to take the reading at 1 p.m., not noon, local time.

Throughout this discussion, I've been using the term local time for good reason. Ever since the late 1800s, the world has been divided into 24 time zones, originally driven by the railroads' need for consistent time at all stations along their routes. Each time zone is 15 degrees wide, and the "standard time" anywhere within a zone is the same. The current time in each successive zone differs by exactly one hour (it's no accident that the sun also moves through a 15-degree arc each hour).

The sun, however, is not due south everywhere in the time zone at the same instant. Only at the longitude line down the center of a zone (the central meridian) is it due south at noon. East of that meridian, the sun is due south earlier than noon; west of it, it's later. "Local noon" is simply defined as the time at which the sun is due south for your current location.

If you're at either edge of a time zone, local noon differs from standard noon by 30 minutes. At the eastern edge, local noon occurs at a standard time of 11:30 a.m. At the western edge, local noon occurs at a standard time of 12:30 p.m. In between, local noon varies depending on how far you are from the central meridian.

If you don't correct for this difference, the direction you determine for due south can be off by 7 degrees or more. Combine that with the fact your watch is probably not perfectly accurate, and your measurement can be off by more than 10 degrees.

Correcting for local time is really quite easy, as long as you know your approximate longitude. Find the difference between your current longitude and the central meridian of your time zone. Then apply the rule of four minutes time difference for each degree of longitude difference. Remember that if you're east of the central meridian, noon comes earlier than standard time, and if you're west it comes later. In the US, the central meridians for each time zone are the following:

Eastern time zone: 75° west longitude
Central time zone: 90° west longitude
Mountain time zone: 105° west longitude
Pacific time zone: 120° west longitude

Here's an example: I'm writing this in Santa Rosa, California, located north of San Francisco in the Pacific time zone at longitude 122° 39′ W. This is 2° 39′ west of the central meridian for this zone. Round this to 2.5° and apply the rule of four minutes time difference for every degree of longitude to get a difference of 10 minutes. Since I'm west of the central meridian, local noon occurs at 12:10 p.m. Pacific Standard Time, or 1:10 p.m. Pacific daylight time.

A few other minor errors arise because the earth's orbit around the sun is not a perfect circle and its axis of rotation is tilted in relation to its orbit. These can account for another 2 to 3 degree error in your measurement. Considering that without map or compass, your ability to navigate a precise bearing is pretty limited anyway, I wouldn't worry about trying to eke out the last degree or two of accuracy in your measurement.

You can slightly improve the accuracy of this technique by sticking a tall, straight pole or stick vertically into level ground and noting the direction of its shadow at local noon. It will be pointing due north.

Equal Height Method

This method is based on the simple fact that the length of a shadow cast by an object such as a stick a certain number of minutes before noon is the same as its length an equal number of minutes after noon. With this method, you don't need to worry about correcting for your longitude, and you don't even need to know exactly when local noon occurs.

You first need to plant an object like a stick, hiking staff, or ski pole into the ground. The surface of the ground must be as level as possible and the stick as close to true vertical as you can make it. At least 30 minutes before local noon, measure the length of the shadow. Lacking a tape measure, you can use your belt or some fishing line, or even a fallen tree

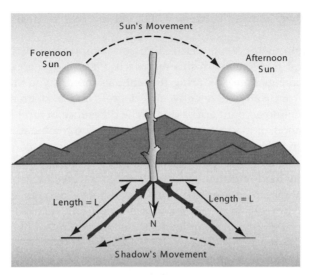

Sun's Movement

Forenoon Sun

Afternoon Sun

Length = L

N

Length = L

Shadow's Movement

Equal height method for determining north: When the length of the shadow after noon equals the length of the shadow before noon, north is halfway between the two directions.

branch, to make the measurement. As you do this, draw a line on the ground to mark the direction of the shadow.

As time progresses, the shadow will get shorter for a time, then begin to lengthen. (If the shadow doesn't get shorter but continues to grow after your initial measurement, you might as well stop, as you've already missed local noon.) Keep measuring the length of the shadow as it grows until it reaches the same length you measured before noon. Immediately draw a new line marking the new direction. North is at an angle halfway between the two lines.

Using Your Watch as a Compass

This is a popular technique reported throughout the literature, but despite the wide press coverage, it's really not very accurate. It's based on the somewhat dubious premise that the sun is directly east at 6 a.m., is directly west at 6 p.m., and is due south at noon. Assuming that to be true, then you should be able to use your analog watch to find south. (If you wear a digital watch, you're pretty much out of luck.)

Here is the procedure: Align your watch so the hour hand is pointed at the sun. This is easiest to do if you hold the watch level and place a slender stick like a match or toothpick vertically in the ground. Align your watch so the shadow falls directly in line with the hour hand.

South is then halfway between 12:00 and the current position of the hour hand.

Recalling the previous discussion, you should immediately recognize several problems with this approach. First, it doesn't correct for daylight savings time, so during the summer months you are immediately in error by anywhere between 7 degrees and 23 degrees. Neither does it take into account errors due to the difference in local noon from standard noon, or inaccuracies in your watch. The combination of these errors, even if you've corrected for daylight savings time, can exceed 20 degrees, relegating this approach to last place on the list.

Other methods are often reported in the literature. If you observe the direction of the sun at sunrise or sunset, you can get a rough approximation of east or west. To get accurate results, though, you need to apply a correction factor from a complicated table that you're not likely to have in your pocket.

Another common but inaccurate method is to place a stick vertically in the ground and watch the direction the shadow moves. This gives you a rough indication of east. But because the sun describes an arc as it moves, the direction is only approximate. Don't expect an accuracy of better than 20 degrees using this technique.

Navigating a Bearing Without a Compass

After you've determined what direction you want to go and where north is, you're ready to start your journey. Now the trick is to navigate that bearing without a compass. The lines you drew in the ground to mark north will be of no help when you're a mile away. And without a reference, most people can't walk a straight line for any distance.

A detailed discussion of the subject is beyond the scope of this book, but here's a tip you might find useful: It's based on the same "common sense" approach to navigation described in Chapter 3, with an additional twist. Pick a point in the distance like a mountain peak or distinctive tree in the direction you want to travel, and use it as a target. Your initial goal will be to hike to that target. Now turn around and pick another object directly behind you to serve as a rear anchor point. It doesn't need to be far away; it can be right nearby. It just needs to be something you'll still be able to see when you reach your first target.

Now imagine a tightrope stretched between this rear anchor point and the target object in front of you. You are the tightrope walker. Your goal is to stay on the tightrope as you walk.

In general, you won't always be able to do this. Undoubtedly, there will be obstacles you have to go around as you hike. Make a point of getting back on the tightrope after you have gone around an obstacle.

You might wonder why you need to worry about tracking a rear anchor point. As long as you can get to your target, why should you care about anything behind you? The problem is that your initial target probably isn't your final goal. When you reach it, you'll need to pick a new target object ahead of you along the same bearing. But since you don't have a compass, how do you know what direction that is?

You could, of course, again use the primitive direction-finding methods described earlier this chapter, but there is an easier way. Look to the rear and locate your anchor point. Now visualize an imaginary line running from it through your current position and continuing forward. Pick a new target along this bearing and continue navigating. You may also need to pick a new anchor point. Continue going, selecting new targets and anchor points as you need them, until you eventually make it back to civilization.

When you don't have a map or compass, knowing how to navigate by visually tracking your surroundings can be the difference between getting to safety and finding yourself farther afield in unknown territory. The time to practice these skills is when you still have a working GPS receiver, not after it's already broken. Whenever you are out with your receiver, consider using the techniques described here to hone your skills in visual navigation.

Part IV
Getting the Most from GPS

Key Concepts

- ▶ All about geocaching

- ▶ Fun things to do with GPS

- ▶ All about track logs

- ▶ How to create accurate trail maps using GPS

- ▶ Using your GPS receiver for highway navigation

- ▶ How to choose a GPS receiver

- ▶ Guide to receivers from popular manufacturers

- ▶ Essential GPS accessories

Geocaching

Geocaching is a fast-growing sport that's a great way to practice GPS navigation skills. The concept is simple: One person hides a container, the "cache," which typically includes a log book, instruction sheet, and a few trading items, and posts its latitude and longitude coordinates on a website. Other people look up the coordinates of the cache (pronounced *cash*) on the web and then use their GPS receivers to try to find it. When they do, they sign the log book and, if they want, take an item. According to geocaching etiquette, if you take an item you must leave another item to replace it. When finished, the cache is returned to its hiding place for others to find.

It sounds easier than it is. Remember, your receiver is typically only accurate to about 20 or 30 feet, and the cache is often camouflaged and small. Your receiver will only get you into the general area. It's up to you to search around until you find it.

Geocaching was unheard of before the government turned off Selective Availability (page 4) in the year 2000. But within days, the first cache was planted in Oregon and the sport was off and running. Now it is a worldwide phenomenon, with caches in nearly 200 countries. Hiding spots range from locations far in the wilderness to downtown urban areas. Geocachers run the gamut from dedicated enthusiasts who hike miles in the backcountry to parents and children who go no farther than the local park.

The first caches were fairly large Army Surplus ammo boxes, but these days, almost any container is used. I've seen fake hollow rocks, magnetic key holders, and just about every kind of plastic or rubber container you can imagine. Hollow logs and rock piles seem to be favorite hiding places. A cache placed in the wilderness need not be well-camouflaged, but in an urban area the biggest challenge is hiding it in a way it won't be found by non-geocachers (called "geomuggles" in geocaching lingo, after the non-magical "muggles" from the Harry Potter stories).

Most caches are placed on public lands, although with the owner's permission they can be placed on private property. Some government

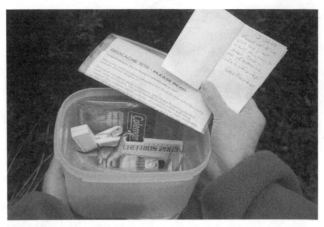

A typical geocache consists of a log book, instruction sheet, and inexpensive trading items housed in a waterproof container.

agencies—viewing geocaches as little more than trash or fearful of potential environmental damage from legions of geocachers tramping willy-nilly over the hillsides—have banned geocaching within their jurisdictions. The National Park Service falls into this category. Other agencies recognize the sport as a way to get more people out to enjoy nature and appreciate their parks. Even public agencies that permit geocaches may require that you obtain a permit first, so before you hide a cache on public land, make sure you are not in violation of any government regulation.

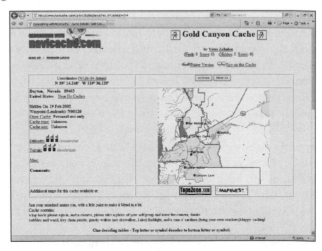

Typical cache page on www.navicache.com (Courtesy of Navicache.com)

Typical cache page on www.geocaching.com (Courtesy of Groundspeak, Inc.)

GEOCACHING WEBSITES

Before you can find a cache, you need to know where to look. The two most important geocaching Internet sites are www.geocaching.com and www.navicache.com. These sites provide the coordinates for thousands of hidden caches. Both provide free access (after you complete a free registration), although Geocaching.com also offers what they call a premium membership that gives you, for a fee, early notification of new caches and access to otherwise unpublished caches. Navicache.com takes a different approach, based on the premise of complete free access to the site. Both provide many opportunities for a good hunt.

If you prefer to find cache coordinates by way of a map rather than entering zip codes or latitudes and longitudes, check out Buxley's Geocaching Waypoint at www.brillig.com/geocaching. This "search engine" page provides map-based links to the caches on Navicache.com and other web pages (legal issues currently prevent links to the Geocaching.com caches).

An Internet search on the words "geocaching" or "geocache" will turn up hundreds of other websites, including regional and international geocaching organizations, upcoming events, and various words of advice. If you're new to the sport, it might be worthwhile to spend a little time browsing a few such sites to learn more about it.

Cache Types

Geocaching is so new, the rules of the game are still evolving. There are several generally accepted types of caches:

Traditional cache. Also called a "normal cache," this original type of cache includes a log book and prizes in a container roughly the size of a breadbox. Army Surplus ammo boxes were the original favorite containers, but too many people considered the boxes themselves to be neat prizes and carted them away. So now you are more likely to see things like Rubbermaid containers, old peanut-butter jars, or empty paint buckets. Caches placed in containers about the size of a 5-gallon paint can are known as "large caches."

Micro cache. Similar to a traditional cache but much smaller. Film canisters, magnetic key holders, and empty breath-mint tins are examples. Often there is little room for anything other than a miniature logbook.

Offset cache. This is a little more complicated than the traditional cache. The published coordinates direct you to some sort of point of interest. You must then continue to a nearby location based on information you learn at the site or from information given on the cache's web page. See the sidebar on page 142 for more information on finding offset caches.

Multipart caches. This requires that you find multiple caches to complete your quest. In one version, several caches are posted on the Internet. Each cache you visit gives you a piece of information necessary to find a final, unpublished cache. In another version, each successive cache gives you coordinates to the next cache in a sequence.

Virtual cache. In urban or heavily traveled rural areas, it isn't always possible to place a physical cache. The base of Yosemite Falls, for example, sees so many visitors it would be impossible to keep a cache hidden for long, even if it weren't against park regulations. A virtual cache gives you the coordinates of a particular point of interest and asks you to answer a question about the location. You email the answer to the "owner" of the cache to prove you were there. This is the only type of cache currently permitted in national parks.

Reverse cache. Also called a "locationless cache," this is the opposite of a traditional cache. Instead of going to a specific waypoint to discover what is there, you are instructed to find a specific type of object and record its coordinates. For more information, visit www.waymarking. com. Public playgrounds, murals, coin-operated binoculars, and suspension bridges are just a few of the many categories you'll find listed at the site.

Other cache types can include puzzle caches, event caches, earth-caches, and letterbox hybrids. Refer to Geocaching.com or Navicache.com for more information.

Difficulty and Terrain

Caches are rated by their owners in terms of difficulty and terrain using a 1-to-5 scale, with 1 being the easiest and 5 the hardest. Difficulty refers to how hard it will be to find the cache, including such factors as the length of the hike and the effort required to find the cache once you get there. Terrain describes the physical nature of the trail to the cache. A rating of 1 indicates the terrain is wheelchair accessible. A rating of 5 indicates a cache that may require specialized equipment such as climbing or scuba gear. Use the ratings as a general guideline—they are assigned subjectively by cache owners, so there can be considerable difference in scoring from one cache to another.

Geocaching Rules

There are four important rules for geocaching:

1. If you take an item from the cache, leave an item. Check rule 6 below for information on what not to put in a cache.

2. Record your visit in the log book.

3. Put the cache back in the same place you found it, unless its instructions say otherwise.

4. Report your visit on the website where you found the coordinates.

If you plan to hide a cache, there are some additional considerations:

5. Include a logbook so visitors can record their experiences. If there's room, include a pencil. If not, be sure your online description of the cache tells people to bring their own.

6. Use common sense when stocking your cache. Never put anything dangerous like fireworks, explosives, ammunition, knives or other weapons, alcohol, illegal substances, or pornography. Remember that geocaching is a family sport and children are often the first to find a cache, so plan accordingly. Food items are also strongly discouraged. Animals are more likely than humans to benefit from such treasures. Besides, would you really want to sample a chocolate bar that may have sat out in the elements for who knows how many months? If you want to provide food, do so with gift certificates for free hamburgers or ice-cream cones at a local restaurant.

7. Never bury a cache. The sport is based on a premise of minimizing environmental impact, so it needs to be placed where it can be found with minimal damage to the environment. (It's OK to cover it loosely with leaves or twigs, but never to the point where it is completely hidden from view.)

8. When you place a cache, you become its "owner." You are responsible for visiting it on occasion to make sure it is in good condition and that the area around it doesn't show signs of overuse. Remove a cache if the environmental impact becomes more than minimal. For this reason, you shouldn't place a cache while on vacation or in a remote area you can't regularly visit.

9. Make sure to record the correct GPS coordinates. Use the WGS 84 datum, and in general, use the degrees-decimal minutes format. Turn on averaging, if available in your receiver, to improve the waypoint's accuracy. Check the rules of the specific website for additional information.

Finding a Cache

If you're new to geocaching, you should practice finding caches to learn the general principles of the sport before you start hiding caches of your own. From the home pages at either Navicache.com or Geocaching.com, you can enter a zip code to get a listing of all caches in the immediate area. The sites also have advanced capabilities that allow you to search on latitude-longitude coordinates, cache names, and several other criteria.

The result of your search will be a list of nearby caches, including hyperlinks to the individual cache pages. Click on a link to learn about a specific cache. Here you will see its latitude-longitude coordinates (Geocaching.com also provides UTM coordinates), learn more about the cache, and read the log notes recorded by previous visitors. Pick a cache that sounds appealing and enter its coordinates into your receiver. Now you're ready to go find it.

If you don't like to manually enter coordinates, Geocaching.com offers a simpler alternative. On the detail page for each cache, just below the cache coordinates, is an icon that allows you to store the cache on your computer as a

Sugarloaf Country
by Daffodil [profile]

N 38° 26.312 W 122° 29.969
UTM: 10S E 543681 N 4254591
E 8.5mi from your home coordinates

Click icon to download:
LOC Waypoint File (*.loc)
Read about waypoint downloads

If you don't like to manually enter waypoint coordinates, www.geocaching.com provides a way to download them directly to your GPS receiver. You first need to install a software application available from the website.

.loc file. Once stored, you can use a program such as EasyGPS to upload the caches to your receiver. The process is quite simple:

1. Go to the Geocaching.com home page, log in, and search for an interesting cache.

2. Call up the home page for the cache. Just below the cache coordinates is an icon labeled "click icon to download." When you click the icon, you are given the choice to open or save the file. Choose "save." A new dialogue box appears that allows you to specify where to save it. It is a good idea to create a separate folder for your caches called something like "geocaches," so if you haven't already done so, create the folder now.

3. Enter a filename and save it to the desired folder. Repeat this process for each cache you want to find.

4. Now open the EasyGPS program (you can download it for free from www.easygps.com). Select the "file" menu and choose each of the waypoints you downloaded.

5. Connect your GPS receiver to the computer (EasyGPS works with either USB or serial ports).

6. Click the "send" icon on the EasyGPS toolbar, confirm the box next to "waypoints" is checked, then select "OK." The caches are transferred to your receiver.

Preparation

The web page for a cache defaults to a high-level map of the surrounding area. It might not be detailed enough to show where to start your hunt. You want to avoid starting from a spot that appears close only to find the way blocked by a canyon, housing development, oil refinery, etc. It's a good idea to study a more detailed map before you head out.

Geocaching.com and Navicache.com both give you the option of displaying the cache location on other online maps including TopoZone, MapQuest, and Microsoft Maps. Topo maps are good bet for caches hidden in rural areas. Street maps are best for urban caches. And this is one area where a mapping receiver really shines. With the right map loaded, your GPS unit can guide you directly from your home to the jumping-off point.

If you're going to a cache that's off the beaten path, you will want to prepare the same way you would for any serious hike. Assemble a backpack with a few basic items: GPS receiver, extra batteries (very important!), magnetic compass, water, snacks, first-aid kit, and perhaps a

FINDING OFFSET CACHES

To find an offset cache, you must first go to the published waypoint coordinates and then perform additional navigation. For example, you may be told that once you reach the waypoint, the cache lies 80 feet away at a bearing of 60 degrees. How do you find it?

Figuring out its direction is fairly easy—use your magnetic compass. Knowing how far to walk is more difficult. Some Garmin receivers have a feature called PROJECT WAYPOINT that allows you to create a new waypoint for a specified bearing and distance away from a stored waypoint. But even if your receiver doesn't have this feature, you can still use it to find the cache. Here's how: First, determine the back bearing of the cache. This is the bearing you would use to walk from the cache back to the published waypoint. If the cache's bearing is less than 180 degrees, find the back bearing by adding 180 degrees to it; if it is greater than 180 degrees, subtract 180 degrees. For instance, if the cache's bearing is 60 degrees, the back bearing would be 240 degrees.

To find the cache, call up the published waypoint, activate the GOTO function, and navigate to it. Once you get there, the cache is 80 feet away at a bearing of 60 degrees. Using your magnetic compass, walk toward the cache, and watch your receiver as the bearing and distance on the screen change. Remember that the bearing you see is the back bearing—the bearing back to the published waypoint—not the bearing to the cache. Keep moving until you are the correct distance and bearing away. In our example, you are at the cache when the published waypoint is 80 feet away from you at a bearing of 240 degrees.

jacket or windbreaker. A cell phone can be handy if you will be within its coverage area. And don't forget to include items you can use to trade. If you plan to be a geocaching regular, you may want to keep the kit together permanently so you can head out at a moment's notice.

Search

It can be just as hard to find the right parking spot for your car as it is to find the cache. Some cache web pages will give you at least an idea of where to start from, but in many cases, you're on your own. If you studied a map before you started, you should be able to get reasonably close.

Park your car and turn on your GPS receiver to get a position fix. The first thing to do, if the cache is any significant distance away, is to mark the location of your car as a waypoint. You don't want to get yourself into the unenviable position of having found the cache but having no idea how to get back. Remember the Cardinal Rule of GPS Navigation: It doesn't do you any good to know where you are if you don't know where you want to go.

By now, you know how to navigate with a GPS receiver, so I won't repeat those instructions here. If you have any questions, now would be a good time to go back and review the basics, starting on page 33.

Many geocachers keep their GPS receivers turned on for the duration of the quest. That way, they can use the compass page as their primary navigation tool. Ever since the demise of Selective Availability, the compass page has become reasonably useful, even at walking speeds. It's still a good idea to carry a magnetic compass as a backup and for use when you are standing still.

Be sure to check the satellite status page occasionally. If you are navigating through forests or canyons, your receiver could lose lock on a satellite or two and drop back into 2D mode. If so, your indicated position could be hundreds of feet away from your actual position. Move around as necessary to keep your receiver operating in 3D mode.

The last 15 to 20 feet are the most challenging. At this point, it's best to put your receiver away—it won't be able to help you now. This is where your search skills become important. Try to imagine where you would have hidden the cache if it were yours. Hollow logs, rock piles, and clumps of brush all make likely hiding spots. The rules of geocaching prohibit buried caches, so don't dig up the ground. But caches are often loosely covered with twigs, small rocks, or dried grass, so check around.

Use common sense when checking concealed spots. It is always possible that snakes, spiders, or scorpions could be lurking within. I've found it useful to carry a hiking staff that I first use to probe such areas. And you should always keep an eye out for poison oak, poison ivy, poison sumac, or whatever other poisonous plants are native to the surrounding area.

At the Cache

Once you've spotted the cache and before you retrieve it, look around to see if anyone else is nearby. You don't want a geomuggle to accidentally discover and pillage the cache after you've left. Wait until it's safe, then retrieve it. Record your visit in the log, swap items if you want, then seal the cache and replace it where you found it. Don't forget to log your visit on the web page when you return home.

Hiding a Cache

Eventually, after you have found a few caches, you may want to hide your own. Re-read the rules for hiding caches on pages 139 and 140, then decide on a plan. At first, you will probably want to keep things simple by hiding a traditional cache. Do some research before hiding it. Are there already other caches nearby? To minimize environmental impact, cache websites usually won't accept new caches placed too close to an existing cache. Also make sure your intended site doesn't violate laws or property rights. Don't place a cache on private property without the owner's permission. On public lands, check with the managing agency if you aren't sure of their policy toward geocaching. Some agencies require that you first obtain a permit before placing a cache.

You'll also have to decide how difficult you want to make the search. A cache that's easy to reach will receive more visits than one placed far in the wilderness. But the challenge of the find can make the wilderness cache a more rewarding experience for those who attempt it. Also give consideration to how the cache is hidden. Don't make people scramble across a delicate natural environment to get to it. The best caches are ones that give the visitor another reason to be there besides the cache—a great scenic view or historical point of interest, for example. Check the website where you plan to post the cache for any additional rules they may have.

Remember, your cache will lie exposed to the weather year round, so choose a container suitable for the environment. If possible, use a plastic or metal container with an airtight seal. Avoid easily broken glass jars. Label the container as a geocache according to instructions on the appropriate web page, so that if it's accidentally found by a geo-muggle, they won't think it's trash and dispose of it.

Travel bug (left) and geocoin (right)

You already know what not to put in a cache, but equally important is what to put in. You don't need to spend a lot of money. Cheap toys are great, since many geocachers are children. Other common items include cash (coins or paper), CDs, DVDs, gift certificates, sunscreen, books, or just about anything else you can think of. Use your imagination. Some cache owners include single-use disposable cameras. The idea is for visitors to take their pictures at the cache and leave the camera there. When all the shots are exposed, the cache owner develops the film and posts the photos on the web.

Travel Bugs and Geocoins

A "travel bug" (also called a hitchhiker) is an item intended to travel from one cache to another. The item can be anything—toys and stuffed animals are favorites—but it is distinguished by a coded metal tag dangling from it. If you take a travel bug from a cache, you're not supposed to keep it, but rather place it in another cache and keep it moving. You also need to log onto the website indicated on the tag to record that you have taken it and to read the instructions the owner has posted for it. The goal might be for the bug to travel around the world or hit as many states as possible in a specific period, so don't hold onto a travel bug for any length of time. As soon as practical, go out to another cache and send it on its way. Then make sure you go to its online log and record where you placed it, so the owner can track its journey.

A geocoin is a custom coin created by an individual or group to be left as a calling card in a geocache. Like a travel bug, a geocoin can have a unique tracking ID, but geocoins are also meant to be kept or traded. When you find a geocoin, be sure to log onto the designated website to see what to do with it. Geocoins have become so popular that numerous companies now create affordable custom coins for geocachers in quantities as small as 100 pieces or less. To learn more, check the Geocoins Information Page at www.geocaching.com/track/geocoin.aspx.

Geocaching can be a great sport for the whole family. Follow the simple guidelines in this chapter, and you will have a good excuse to get outside with your GPS receiver more often.

12

More Fun and Games

Once you are comfortable with your GPS receiver, you'll undoubtedly want to find new ways to use it, if for no other reason than to justify to the rest of your family why you bought it. In this chapter, we'll give you a few ideas for fun things to do with your receiver, starting with solo activities and finishing up with team games. Don't be afraid to use these ideas as starting points to invent your own variations.

Track Log Maps

The previous chapters focused on how to use a GPS receiver to get you to a destination. But your receiver also excels at another task—recording the route you took to get there. All receivers designed for the outdoors can generate a track log, or detailed record of the path you took to get from a starting point to a destination. You'll often hear it described as a "bread-crumb trail," in reference to the old story of Hansel and Gretel.

Track logs as displayed on the eTrex (left) and Vista (center). At right, the eTrex track log has been downloaded to a USGS map using Topo! software. This clearly shows how some park trails have been relocated from their original routes to reduce environmental impact on sensitive meadows. (Map created with Topo! ©2006 National Geographic)

But unlike poor Hansel's bread crumbs, which were eaten by birds, your receiver's track log remains in memory until you explicitly delete it.

Track Back Feature

A track log can be valuable in many ways. In the simplest case, you can use it to retrace your exact path back to a starting point. (In contrast, following a waypoint bearing only shows you the straight-line path to a destination.) Simply turn on your receiver, activate the track log feature before you start out, and let your receiver keep track of your path. Every time you pass a threshold in either time or distance from the last log point, another point is automatically added. This continues until you either complete your journey or the track log memory gets filled. Memories typically range from 1000 to 10,000 points, so even the smallest memory should be sufficient to record a journey of a few hours or more.

Be sure to clear your receiver's track log memory before you start out, and keep your receiver turned on for the entire time. That way you'll get a complete record of your path without any extraneous information. When you are ready to return, go to the map page and zoom in enough to get a detailed view of the track. Then just follow the track back to your origin. Many receivers make the job easier by providing a "track back" feature that creates a route from your track. Your receiver generates a number of phantom waypoints from the stored track log and connects them just like any other route.

Using a Track Log with a Computer

Perhaps more interesting is the fact that a track log allows you to store a complete record of your journey for future reference. Once your receiver has recorded a track log, you can download it to a computer where you can display and analyze it on a software map. This kind of mapping is so useful that all of Chapter 13 is devoted to showing you how to make the most accurate maps. If you don't need that level of accuracy and just want to log a record of your journey, the following paragraphs give you a simplified overview.

To create an accurate track log, the receiver must have a clear view of the sky the entire time. This eTrex is mounted to the shoulder strap of a backpack.

First, for your receiver to capture an uninterrupted log, you must leave it turned on for the entire journey. Make sure your batteries are fresh and always carry spares. You must also make sure your receiver doesn't lose satellite lock as you travel, so don't bury it in a pocket or backpack. Keep it out where it has a clear view of the sky and its antenna is correctly oriented. This is one situation where an external antenna is useful so you can store the receiver in your pocket or backpack and keep only the antenna visible. I've had good success with a Garmin GPSmap 60CSx and

If you're handy with tools, you can make a custom clip that allows you to attach an external antenna to your clothing.

an external antenna. I designed a custom clip so I can easily attach the antenna to my shirt. I've also been successful placing it inside a hat. Tilley (www.tilley.com) makes several hats with a pocket that can hold the antenna inside the crown. I run the cable under my shirt to be less conspicuous.

Another thing to remember is that a track log remains in memory until you explicitly clear it, so before you start a new journey, clear any existing data from previous trips. Otherwise, the old data and the new will all be recorded as a continuous jumble of information. You usually clear the track log from the SETUP page, although on some receivers you do it from the MAP page.

Finally, remember your receiver has only a fixed amount of track log memory. In most cases, it takes at least several hours to fill up, but when it does get filled, your receiver starts overwriting the oldest data with the newest. (You can usually also select an option to stop recording when the memory is full.) The TRACK LOG screen shows you what percentage of the memory has been used.

Some receivers let you store the active track to a separate memory. If your receiver lets you do this, you'll want to store it when the track log memory approaches 100 percent, then start a new log. You can later download all the stored tracks into a computer, where they can be joined and analyzed as a single record. This option isn't available in less expensive receivers that have only a single track log memory. Note that most receivers don't save a stored track at full resolution, so if that's important to you, don't delete it from the active track log.

You can select several options when creating a track log. The most useful is the "automatic" mode, where the receiver decides when your position has changed enough to justify adding another point to the track. It is smart enough to know that if you're driving on the freeway at 60 miles per hour, there can be more distance between points than if you are walking a trail at 2 miles per hour.

You typically also have two other options: Store points at either a constant time interval or a specific distance from the previous point. In almost all cases, you are better off leaving your receiver set to automatic mode.

Before you can do anything with the track log, you need to get it out of your receiver and into your computer. For this, you need a software mapping program like those described in Chapter 6. A program like National Geographic Topo! or Maptech Terrain Navigator makes it easy to import the track log directly onto a map so you can see precisely where you have traveled.

Using track logs, you can do such things as chart the course of a river or design the route of a marathon race. These are fairly obvious applications, but there are others as well. I know one author of hiking guidebooks who uses this approach to make accurate records of trail routes and distances for his books. Another avid mountain biker friend used his GPS receiver to plot a 40-mile course through a nearby state park. He then rode the course to celebrate his 40th birthday—and swears he'll continue matching distance to age every 10 years until he turns 80!

GPS Golf

A good part of a successful golf game is knowing the correct club to use for the current distance to the green. This is a great potential use of GPS. There are many commercial GPS-based golfing systems you can rent or buy, but it is also possible to use a standard GPS receiver. You first have to store as GPS waypoints the positions of all the greens and any other points of interest (sand traps, water hazards, etc.). Then when you are on the course, simply use the GOTO function to determine your distance from the green or hazard. Remember that most receivers report distance in feet, so you'll have to mentally divide the answer by three to convert it to yards.

The roughly 20-foot accuracy of standard GPS is somewhat marginal for golf. Newer receivers with WAAS capability can bring this down to a more acceptable 2-yard error or less—if you can lock onto a WAAS signal. Fortunately, most golf courses are fairly wide open spaces, so your chances of picking up a WAAS satellite are better than average.

You might wonder how you go about storing the various waypoints. If you regularly play the same course, you can store the important waypoint locations during one round so you can use them in later rounds.

You might also consider trading this information with others who have recorded different courses.

Find the Flags

This is a group exercise I often use with students in my GPS navigation classes. It takes a little advance preparation, but the results are well worth it. The exercise works best for groups of between six and 12 people, and you'll need several GPS receivers. You'll also need access to a fairly large open area such as a state or regional park that doesn't get a lot of traffic. (Make sure you use a park where it is permissible to hide objects for later recovery.)

The concept is fairly straightforward. A day or so before the game, one person—the master of ceremonies—goes into the park and hides a number of objects (I use small flags of the type landscapers use to mark the locations of sprinkler heads), being certain to accurately record their coordinates as GPS waypoints. The master of ceremonies should hide the flags so they are not likely to be discovered accidentally by strangers, while avoiding unwarranted environmental impact or hazards such as poison oak. On the day of the game, the group gathers at the designated meeting spot and the master of ceremonies hands out waypoint coordinates.

It works best if the group is divided into several teams of two or three people each, depending on the number of GPS receivers available. As a minimum, one person from each team needs a GPS receiver while the others should at least have magnetic compasses so they can follow the indicated GPS bearings. Each team competes against all the other teams to be the first to find specific flags.

For a group of 12 people, I typically hide 10 flags. The group is organized into four teams of three people each. Each team receives coordinates for two of the 10 flags, plus a sealed envelope containing the coordinates of the final two flags. Each team must program the coordinates into their receivers and go search for their two assigned flags. Only after they have found their assigned flags can a team open the envelope and begin the search for the final two flags, which all teams are competing to find. The first team to find their two assigned flags plus the final two flags is declared the winner.

Depending on skill levels, you can make the game more or less complicated. For novices, you should stick to a common datum and position format for all waypoints. For more skilled groups, you might want to list some waypoints in degrees-minutes-seconds format and others in degrees-decimal minutes format. You might also want to reference some to WGS 84 and others to NAD 27 (or even some exotic datum like

Easter Island 1967, as long as you know it works in your region and that everyone's receiver includes it as a choice).

It's best if you can place flags at least 100 feet apart so that everyone isn't stumbling over each other as they search. You'll also want to keep in mind the athletic ability of the individuals. I typically place flags about a quarter to a half mile from the starting point and assign the more athletic members of the group to find the more distant flags. Consider other details, too. The master of ceremonies is responsible for helping any teams that get into difficulty. Inexpensive, two-way radios can be useful communications tools during the hunt and to help the master of ceremonies steer a team in the right direction if they start diverging from their goal. A prize such as a bottle of wine or picnic lunch at the end can serve as ample motivation.

GPS Team Building

Here's an exercise I sometimes use with company executives as part of a leadership training program. It is also useful for youth groups or athletic teams who must understand the value of cooperation. In industry, managers must learn that their business will be successful only if two things happen: If each individual department is successful on its own, and if all departments work toward a common goal. This exercise is designed to drive home both of those points.

It is somewhat similar to "Find the Flags." A group of between six and 15 people is divided into several teams of two or three members each. There must be at least one GPS receiver for each team. A reasonably large open space such as a park is also essential. A day or two ahead of time, I hide several objects in the park and record their waypoint coordinates. But instead of hiding flags, I use small plastic containers. The number of containers is one more than the number of teams—if there are three teams, for example, I hide four containers.

The last container is the ultimate goal. It is the objective that everyone is working toward. It might contain a small reward—coupons that can be redeemed for food, drink, or some memento of the program, for instance. Each of the other containers includes two things: the name of a second waypoint location and a clue to the location of the final container. Each team must find their assigned initial container, then go to the second waypoint. There is no hidden treasure at this location; it is just a meeting point. The idea is that all teams converge at this point and piece together the clues to find the last container. Only if each team is successful individually can the entire group reach the final goal.

Keep in mind that if you're doing this with GPS novices, you won't want to take the time to teach them the subtleties of position formats or map datums. It's best if you program all the waypoints into all the receivers ahead of time, then just give the teams the waypoint names and teach them how to use the GOTO function. The clues can then simply consist of parts of the final waypoint's name.

I generally keep the instructions fairly vague. Players learn how to use the GOTO function, and they learn the location of their initial container. But they are on their own to figure out what to do after that. Part of the challenge is figuring out why you are at the second waypoint and what to do when you get there.

Make sure to program the coordinates of every waypoint into every GPS receiver. That way, a team that has successfully found its clue has the option of helping another team that is struggling. Whether or not they actually think to do that is up to them. I normally wouldn't offer that advice ahead of time but rather let them figure it out for themselves as part of learning to work together. Once again, inexpensive, handheld, two-way radios can be useful tools to help the teams communicate with each other.

Orienteering: GPS Relay Race

Orienteering is a competitive sport in which you find your way as quickly as possible across wilderness terrain to a series of control points using only a map and compass. It is usually a solo sport where GPS receivers are expressly prohibited, although GPS-based events are becoming more common. Here's a similar, team-oriented idea that relies on GPS skills rather than map-reading skills. It consists of a relay race in which each contestant uses a GPS receiver to navigate to where the next team member is waiting. It is particularly suited to runners, bicyclists, or cross-country skiers. You will need a receiver for each participant.

Start with two or more teams of four contestants each. Every contestant needs a GPS receiver. Well in advance of race day, the race organizer must design the course. City streets or backcountry trails work equally well. Unlike true orienteering, no topo map is involved. Instead, contestants are given GPS waypoint coordinates and must use their skill and judgment to find the best route.

In designing the course, consider the type of competition. If it is a foot race, each leg might be a mile or two long. For cyclists, it could be 5 miles or more. Plot a closed-loop course—one that ends where it began. Identify three spots along the way at roughly equal intervals and record these locations as GPS waypoints. These will be the relay exchange points. Don't let any of the participants know these locations ahead of time.

On race day, each member of the team except the first contestant receives the starting and ending coordinates for his or her leg of the race.

The starting contestant is given the coordinates for the complete list of waypoints. His GPS receiver will serve as the "baton" that is passed between each relay member. Its track log will prove that it traversed the entire course, so it must be cleared before starting the race.

Prior to the start, team members must individually enter the waypoints for their leg of the race into their receiver. To make it more challenging, these waypoints should not be shared with other team members. Contestants then find their way to the starting points of their own legs, where they will wait for the handoff. Depending on distance and terrain, they may get there by walking, driving, or bicycling as appropriate.

Give the contestants enough time to get into position (15 to 30 minutes should be ample), then start the race. The first contestants must get to the waypoint at the end of their leg by following any route they choose. If all goes well, when they arrive, they will meet the second contestant and exchange GPS receivers. Of course, this depends on both contestants having accurately programmed the waypoint coordinates and having accurately navigated to the correct position. Assuming a successful transfer, the race continues through all the legs until the final contestant reaches the finish line carrying the GPS receiver that traversed the entire route. At the end of the race, the track log from this receiver can be downloaded to a computer to confirm it was taken to all of the intermediate waypoints without shortcutting. After completing their individual legs, the other contestants can use the exchanged receivers to find their way back to the starting point.

To make it more competitive, different teams shouldn't follow the same route at the same time. If there are only two teams and the geography is uniform, consider having them run the same course in opposite directions. If more than two teams are involved, use staggered starting times.

Organized Activities

You can easily invent variations on the games in this chapter such as combined events involving running, cycling, skiing, and more. Search the web for such topics as "GPS orienteering" to see what events might already be established in your local area. Geocaching is currently the most popular organized GPS activity, but new games regularly pop up on the internet. For example, "geodashing" is a game in which a large number of waypoints throughout the world are posted on the geodashing web page at geodashing.gpsgames.org. The object is to reach the most waypoints before the game ends. "Waymarking" (www.waymarking.com) is a game in which your goal is to find specific types of objects and record their GPS coordinates for others to see. Various other games can be found at gpsgames.org.

Trail Mapping with GPS

G PS receivers are ideally suited for creating maps of hiking, biking, and vehicular trails. Simply leave your receiver turned on while you follow the trail, and it will store a complete record of your journey. When you return home, download the data from your GPS receiver into a mapping software program such as National Geographic Topo! or OziExplorer to plot the trail on a topo map or aerial photograph. This chapter describes how to use your GPS receiver to accurately create custom maps.

Limitations

The first thing to understand is that with a consumer-grade receiver, you won't get the kind of survey-grade accuracy you can achieve with a specialized receiver from a manufacturer such as Trimble or Leica. A survey-grade receiver costs $3000 to $10,000 and can do several things a consumer unit can't. First, it usually has built-in differential correction (DGPS) capability that can improve accuracy from 7 to 15 meters to less than 1 meter (WAAS in a consumer receiver has similar performance, if you can receive the satellite signals). And with access to the appropriate post-processing software, you can even get centimeter accuracy.

Second, a survey-grade unit can automatically record the instantaneous accuracy associated with each track point. When you walk under tree cover and lose satellite lock, the survey-grade receiver flags those data points and allows you to eliminate them from the final record. A consumer receiver, on the other hand, records every track point as if it were just as accurate as every other point, so you have to manually identify regions where you lost satellite lock.

Finally, with the survey-grade receiver, the track log can be downloaded as a series of lines and arcs— called a "shapefile"—that are useful in advanced GIS (geographic information system) mapping software programs such as Arcview. The consumer receiver simply records your path as a series of individual dots. (It is possible to convert track logs from Garmin receivers into shapefiles using third-party software. For more information, refer to the Minnesota Department of Natural

Resources web page at www.dnr.state.mn.us/mis/gis/tools/arcview/extensions/DNRGarmin/DNRGarmin.html.)

For trail-mapping purposes, these limitations may not be significant. If you plan to plot the trail on a USGS 7.5-minute topo map, for example, a 7- to 15-meter error is hardly noticeable. It amounts to less than half a millimeter on the final map—about the width of the line used to represent the trail. Shapefiles are important for highway engineers who need very accurate representations of roads, but they are rarely essential for creating recreational trail maps. And if you are attentive while walking the trail, you can manually identify less accurate sections of the track log and adjust them later when creating the final map.

Advance Planning

Before starting out, you need a plan. If you merely want to walk a trail and record your route, the plan can be simple. But if you want to do things like measure distances between trail junctions, mark the locations of points of interest, or identify areas of the trail that need repair, you need a more detailed plan. Professionals not only record the route of the trail, they also record such information as the trail width, grade, surface type, and the locations of bridges, streams, buildings, signposts, fences, gates, and other points of interest.

This information can be classified into two categories: points and lines (a third category, area, is less important for trail mapping). A signpost, for example, is a point. Its location is recorded as a single waypoint. Trail width is an example of a line. A certain section of the trail may be a single-track footpath, while another section may be a dirt fire road. You would mark the starting and ending points of each section as separate waypoints, together with notes about the trail width along each section.

You can imagine that if you intend to do a detailed survey of a trail, you will end up storing lots of waypoints. It is not unusual for a professional to store many hundreds of data points along a 20-kilometer trail. Although you probably won't need that many, it is still wise to use a receiver with the ability to store at least 1000 waypoints.

Unless you are making a very simple trail map, you will need to take detailed notes along the way. These should include the waypoint name, its distance from the trailhead (as read from the GPS odometer), and specific information about why the waypoint was recorded. You may also want to record repeating information for each waypoint, such as the trail width or surface condition at that waypoint. Some GPS receivers allow you to enter a note with the waypoint, but this tends to be a tedious way to record the data and may not allow you to record enough information. You'll probably want a paper log such as the example log sheet shown here.

Trail Name:_____ ID:_____

Trail Mapping Record

Date:			Mapped by:	
Waypoint	Distance	Surface	Width	Notes

Trailhead	Trail Junction	Picnic Area	Water Source
Entering Tree Cover	Campground	Parking Area	Point of Interest
Leaving Tree Cover	Restroom	Bridge	Sign/Monument

Many GPS receivers allow you to specify a symbol when marking a waypoint. This can be useful in helping group similar waypoints as you are creating the final map. The Garmin GPSmap 60Cx, for example, allows you to select from dozens of symbol types in such categories as Outdoors, Points of Interest, Markers, Marine, Civil, Transportation, Navaids, and Signs. You may want to create a list of the different feature types you intend to record and the symbol you will use for each feature. These could include trail junctions, bridges, points of interest, signposts, gates, a change in trail width or surface, etc. The symbol choices in the GPS receiver won't necessarily match up with what you need—you probably won't find a "gate" symbol, for example—but don't worry. Just pick one of the existing symbols and use it whenever you reach a gate. Of course, you will need to remember to select the right symbol each time you mark a waypoint, something that can become tedious if you record many different types of features.

Finally, you'll need to recognize that if you intend to be serious about it, you will need to devote all your attention to mapping the trail. Don't expect to hike it in record time, nor should you expect to do much sightseeing or exploration along the way. Your objective is to travel the trail with no deviations, and you can't afford to be distracted by various detours as you go. If the trail allows, you'll cover distance more quickly on horseback, on a mountain bike, or on an ATV. One advantage of walking, though, is that you will be less tempted to rush past a feature you should have marked as a waypoint.

Think twice about making it a family outing. Spouses and children will quickly get bored stopping every few hundred feet to record a new feature, and you'll soon find it impossible to do an accurate job. If you do bring others along, make sure they are active participants—taking notes, watching for features to be recorded, and helping navigate through regions of poor satellite reception. You will appreciate the extra help.

Recommended Equipment

While most consumer GPS receivers can be used for trail mapping, not every one will work. Here are the things to consider if you are in the market to make a purchase:

Computer Interface. The track log doesn't do any good sitting inside the GPS receiver. You have to transfer it to a computer. So you absolutely must use a receiver that can be connected to a computer. This might seem obvious, but be aware that some receivers, most notably the less expensive models in the Magellan eXplorist and Lowrance iFinder

Equipment for creating trail maps (clockwise from top left): GPS receiver, external antenna, pedometer, magnetic compass

lines, don't have this ability. If you expect to do a lot of trail mapping, you may also want to consider a model with a fast USB interface. the Garmin GPSmap 60 series, the eTrex Vista C/Legend C, or the Magellan eXplorist 400/500/600, for example.

Sensitive receiver. While no receiver is perfect, a more sensitive receiver will maintain better satellite lock in difficult conditions such as under tree cover or in hilly terrain. Receivers that use the SiRFstarIII chip from SiRF Technology or the Hammerhead chip from Global Locate will perform better in difficult conditions.

Large track log memory. The larger the memory, the longer you can go before filling up the track log memory. The Garmin GPSMAP 60Cx, with 10,000 track log points, is a good choice. The Magellan eXplorist 400/500/600 have unlimited track point storage via removable SD card, but their less sensitive antennas are a disadvantage when you're navigating under tree cover.

External antenna. Your GPS receiver must maintain satellite lock the entire time you are navigating the trail, and satellite signals can't travel through your body. The best solution is to use an external antenna mounted on the top of your head (or hidden discreetly under the crown of a hat). You can then hold the receiver comfortably at your side and monitor the strength of the satellite signals without fear of blocking them. Receivers that can work with an optional external antenna include the Garmin GPSmap 60Cx, GPSmap 76Sx, and the discontinued Magellan Meridian.

Long battery life/outdoor viewable screen. You'll probably be out on the trail for many hours. You need a rugged receiver designed for extended outdoor use, and one that allows you to replace batteries in the field. You also want a screen display that can easily be read outdoors. These requirements alone pretty much eliminate PDA-based receivers.

For serious work, avoid any receiver that can't be used with an external antenna. Place the antenna inside a hat (Tilley hats have a handy pocket inside the crown that can be used for this) and run the cable underneath your clothing to the GPS receiver in your pocket or attached to your belt. Except for the small amount of cable that might be visible running down the back of your neck, it is pretty inconspicuous, and it keeps your hands free for other things.

You will also need a magnetic compass. Aside from helping you keep from getting lost if your GPS receiver fails, it is useful in determining trail bearings in areas of heavy tree cover where the GPS receiver loses satellite lock. This use is covered shortly.

Finally, you may want to bring along a separate mechanical pedometer. It will be useful in measuring distances along stretches of the trail where the GPS receiver loses satellite lock.

Recording Track Logs in the Field

The following step-by-step instructions describe how to create trail maps suitable for such uses as park maps or hiking guidebooks. Remember, you can't expect to generate survey-grade maps with a consumer GPS receiver.

1. At the trailhead, take care of all incidental matters (putting on a backpack, saddling horses, visiting the restroom, etc.) before turning

on your GPS receiver. Ensure that you have collected everything you need, including notebook, magnetic compass, spare batteries, water bottle, food, first-aid kit, etc.

2. Ensure that the batteries in your receiver are fresh, and that you are carrying spares. Turn on the receiver and wait for it to enter 3D mode by locking onto at least four satellites. Confirm the map datum is set correctly (normally WGS 84) and that the coordinate display is set to the desired format (typically either degrees-decimal minutes or UTM).

3. Although not absolutely essential, it is best to delete all existing waypoints from the receiver's memory. That way, at the conclusion of the trip, the only waypoints will be the ones you have stored along the way.

4. Only when you are standing at the trailhead and are ready to depart should you mark the trailhead as a GPS waypoint, making sure to select the appropriate waypoint symbol. If your receiver has way-point averaging capability, activate it and remain stationary for at least three minutes before saving the waypoint. If you previously deleted all existing waypoints from your receiver's memory, it is fine to just save it with the default waypoint number 001 and go up from there. If you didn't, you will need to give each waypoint a unique name. Record the waypoint information on your log sheet.

5. Once you have marked the trailhead, clear the track log, reset the odometer, confirm the track log function is turned on, and start the journey. Check the map page to make sure you are recording a track log, but otherwise leave the display set to the satellite page so you can easily monitor satellite signal strengths.

6. Whenever you reach a feature of interest, stop. Mark it as a way-point, remembering to select the appropriate symbol. Use waypoint averaging, if available, and record the details of the feature on your log sheet.

7. Keep the GPS receiver turned on all the time, and don't wander away from the trail. If you must make a detour for some reason, first turn off the receiver. Then return to the exact point of departure before turning it back on. Wait for it to acquire 3D lock before moving.

8. While traveling, keep an eye on the satellite signal strength bars. If you drop out of 3D mode into 2D mode (tracking only three satellites), immediately mark the location as a waypoint. Mark another waypoint when you again return to 3D mode. The GPS track log in this region may not be accurate, and you may need to make adjustments to it on the computer. As you travel this portion of the trail,

carefully note how it runs. Is it straight, or does it make sudden turns? Record your observations in the logbook. Use your magnetic compass to note the bearing of the trail and how it changes as you move. Use the mechanical pedometer to measure distances along this portion of the trail. When you transfer the track log into your computer, carefully examine this portion, looking for deviations that don't correlate with your live observations. Manually adjust the GPS track log if necessary.

9. If you completely lose lock and can't even maintain 2D mode, immediately return to the location where you last achieved lock. Mark it as a waypoint and note in your log that this is where you lost lock. One of the disadvantages of a consumer GPS receiver is that when you lose lock, it doesn't immediately tell you. Instead, for about 30 seconds or so, it assumes you are continuing at the same speed and direction as you were when you lost lock. It extrapolates the track log in this direction for a few hundred feet, even if you have stopped (it gets worse the faster you were traveling at the time). If it doesn't reacquire satellites within about 30 seconds, it finally stops recording and tells you that it has lost lock. While this feature may not annoy the casual user, it can play havoc with trail mapping, as it results in phantom portions of the track log that have no relation to reality. Again, use your magnetic compass to record the trail bearings and your mechanical pedometer to record the length of each segment in this region. Mark another waypoint when you reacquire lock. After downloading the final track log into your computer, you will have to manually delete these inaccurate regions and use your written records to reconstruct this portion of the trail.

10. If your trail is an open-loop route (one in which you return along the same path as you went out), you may want to record the return path as well as the outbound track. If your GPS receiver allows you to save track logs, you might consider saving the outbound track log, then clearing it from the active track log and resetting the odometer before returning. That way, you have a completely independent record of the return trip. You can later overlay both tracks in the computer to observe how well they align. However, most GPS receivers simplify the track logs when saved, so if you want to maintain full resolution, don't clear it from the active track log. There is no need to again record all the previously stored features, though you could discover and mark additional features you missed on the outbound leg.

11. At the end of the trip, save the track log in memory so you don't ac-
    cidentally overwrite it later (but don't clear it from the active track
    log). Check over your notes and make necessary clarifications now
    while they are still fresh in your mind.

Creating the Final Map

Once you have recorded the track log and waypoints, there are several
ways to create a final map using commercially available mapping software. The exact details of how to use any specific software program
are beyond the scope of this book, so this section will focus on general
methods. Let's assume you are using consumer-grade mapping software such as National Geographic Topo! or OziExplorer, rather than
full-featured—and very expensive—GIS software.

The advantage of a self-contained program like Topo! is that it includes topographic maps. This is great if it includes the map for your
area of interest, but it's useless if your trail lies outside the map borders.
You can currently obtain Topo! software for any of the 50 states, as well
as certain other areas such as national parks. Its highest-resolution maps
are scanned versions of USGS 7.5-minute maps. Unlike paper maps,
Topo! provides seamless coverage of the entire park or state.

OziExplorer doesn't include maps. You must obtain them separately,
either from OziExplorer or from a third-party source. The advantage to
this is that with the right map, OziExplorer works for any region in the
world. It also works with aerial photographs. Once you have calibrated
the map or photo in OziExplorer, you can then accurately display track
logs and waypoints on it.

The following process makes use of Topo! software to create maps
suitable for publication. You can use a similar approach with OziExplorer.

Download the waypoints and track log from the GPS receiver into
Topo!. Delete any downloaded waypoints or track logs that are not part
of the current project.

Export the Topo! map to a jpeg file using the PRINT MAP function.
Select the print boundaries to cover the area of interest without including more than necessary. If you have many waypoints, you may need to
export two versions, one including the waypoints and a less cluttered
version showing only the track log. This is where waypoint symbols can
be useful. Since you probably won't need to show every type of waypoint on the final map, you can minimize the clutter by exporting only
the waypoints with the desired symbols.

For some applications, this jpeg file may be sufficient, although the
resulting map has rather low resolution. It is also cluttered with many

Intermediate steps in creating the final trail map using National Geographic Topo! software: Above, the track log and waypoints have been downloaded to Topo! and the resulting map exported as a jpeg file. In some cases, this level of quality may be sufficient. Note the file includes a scale bar at the bottom.

Below, the jpeg file has been imported into Adobe Illustrator and the features are being traced. Note that the water, which will be gray in the final map, and the land, which will be white, have been set to semitransparent so the underlying jpeg file can still be seen. (Map created with Topo! ©2006 National Geographic)

Final map after deleting the jpeg file and resetting the opacity of fill areas to 100 percent. Legend and scale information have been included, and waypoints have been labeled. This map also includes index contour lines. The resulting map is clean and easy to read.

features, such as contour lines, structures, and shading you may not want to show in the final map. In this case, you can use a drawing program like Adobe Illustrator to create a simplified map by tracing over only the important features.

Here's how to create a map in Adobe Illustrator. Other graphics programs work similarly:

1. Launch Adobe Illustrator, create a blank page, and import the jpeg file into it. If you know how to use layers, create a specific layer for the jpeg bitmap.

2. Trace over the trail and important features (roads, shorelines, park boundaries, etc.) using the line and polygon drawing tools. Again, if you know how to use layers, create a separate layer or layers on top of the bitmap layer for the tracings, and keep all the layers locked except for the one you are currently working on. While tracing, any filled areas you create should be set to be semi-transparent, at about 20 percent to 50 percent opacity. That way you can still see the underlying jpeg image. Once you have finished tracing, you can set opacity back to 100 percent.

3. If the track log has anomalies from losing satellite lock, adjust the traced line to best represent the actual trail. Refer to your written notes to help reconstruct these portions of the trail.

4. Mark the locations of any exported waypoints you want to appear on the final map.

5. Topo! includes a map scale at the bottom of the jpeg file. Be sure to include a tracing of this in the final map.

6. Use the text tool to add labels where you want them.

7. It is not usually necessary to copy the contour lines, because the final map could look too cluttered. If contour lines are desired, you may want to trace over only the index contours.

8. After you are finished, delete the underlying jpeg file. You will be left with a clean representation of the trail and its relevant surroundings. Refer to the accompanying illustrations on pages 164 and 165 to get a better idea of how to do this.

Highway Navigation with GPS

Before you can explore the outdoors, you first have to get there. In the past, that meant fumbling with an oversize paper highway map. Today, you may prefer to use your GPS receiver instead. When loaded with a map of local roads and highways, it can be a great navigational tool to get you to your starting point, whether it be a distant trailhead or nearby geocache. More expensive receivers can even give turn-by-turn navigation instructions to guide you as you drive.

GPS receivers for highway navigation come in two flavors: those intended expressly for use in a vehicle, and those intended primarily for the outdoors. The former have large displays, detailed nationwide road maps, and, most importantly, the ability to provide voice-prompted, turn-by-turn driving instructions. But they don't have the features necessary for outdoor navigation.

The latter are not optimized for use in a vehicle. The displays are much smaller and they don't provide voice guidance. When you approach a turn, they typically beep and display written driving instructions. This makes it unsafe for a driver to navigate alone; it's a two person job. The driver needs to focus on the road while the navigator reads the GPS display and gives the driving instructions. If you're not willing to do this, don't use your outdoor receiver for highway navigation; the hazard to yourself and others is too great. Instead, buy a separate, in-vehicle system complete with a soothing, synthesized voice to guide you along your way.

With either type of receiver, you need to use common sense

The Lowrance iWAY 600c is a GPS receiver designed expressly for highway navigation. It can display highway maps on top of satellite images of the earth. (Courtesy of Lowrance)

and not blindly trust the displayed instructions. Roads may have changed since the software map was created, or current construction may force you to change plans. And remember that the receiver doesn't know the details of the neighborhoods it directs you through. I once used a handheld, auto-routing GPS receiver as my sole navigation tool on a weeklong business trip throughout the East Coast. It worked flawlessly the entire time until one late night when it directed my colleague and me through the seediest part of a run-down New Jersey suburb, apparently because it was the shortest route to our destination.

Highway Navigation Basics

Highway navigation with GPS is nothing more than a special version of a multileg route. The "waypoints" for the route are the road intersections where you must make a turn. You navigate from one intersection to the next until you reach your destination.

If you don't have a mapping receiver, you can still do it, but it is a fairly cumbersome process. You must first figure out the route, then manually place a waypoint at the location of each turn. You'll need to place the waypoints using a software program such as Garmin's MapSource MetroGuide, Magellan's MapSend DirectRoute, or Lowrance's MapCreate. You then create a route and transfer both waypoints and route to your receiver.

To create the waypoints, launch the program and zoom in on the desired area. Use the program's waypoint tool to place waypoints at the important intersections (you may not want to mark every turn, just the key locations). It's best to name them consecutively, starting from 001 so there is no confusion about their order when you create the route.

Although the Lowrance iFinder H2Oc does not provide turn-by-turn guidance, it does allow you to look up street addresses and display their locations on the screen.

Once you have placed the waypoints, you are ready to create the route. Open the route page in the computer software program and add each waypoint to it in succession. When finished, connect your receiver to the computer and transfer both waypoints and route to it. Once in your receiver, you can activate the route and navigate it just like any other route.

It sounds plausible, but in reality, you will rarely find it practical for any but the simplest routes. Even driving a fairly short distance may include a dozen or more turns, and it quickly becomes tedious to manually create the necessary waypoints. Another problem is that the standard route function in a GPS receiver is designed more for hiking than driving. It doesn't tell you what to do next until you are almost at the waypoint. When driving, that's a problem. Do you turn left or right at the next intersection? Which lane do you need to be in to make the turn? You need to know this long before you get there, and the advantage of a receiver with turn-by-turn guidance is that it prompts you well in advance.

With a non-mapping receiver, the best way to do highway navigation is to create a printed list of driving instructions using a free Internet mapping program such as MapQuest (www.mapquest.com) or Google Maps (maps.google.com). In either program, you type in a starting and ending address to get a complete list of driving directions. Alternatively, if you own a software mapping program such as Garmin's City Navigator or Magellan's DirectRoute, you can use it to get a similar list of driving directions. You may want to load your GPS receiver with the latitude-longitude coordinates of a few key intersections (obtained from a suitable mapping program) to help keep you from getting completely lost, but the printed driving directions will serve as your primary navigation tool.

One step up from a non-mapping receiver is a mapping receiver that shows roads and highways but doesn't have the capability for turn-by-turn navigation guidance. The Lowrance iFinder H2Oc and the grayscale-display version of the Garmin eTrex Vista are examples of this type of receiver. The iFinder H2Oc can even look up an address for you and show it on the map. This is a definite advantage if your destination is a street address or other point of interest, but it may not be as helpful if you're heading out to find a geocache.

When the iFinder H2Oc is loaded with detailed street-level maps from MapCreate, you can place waypoints on the map by looking up an address or moving the cursor to the desired location and pushing ENTER. You must then create the route by adding waypoints to it in sequence, as described earlier. Since it can't give turn-by-turn guidance, this type of receiver is best used with printed driving directions. One advantage it affords, though, is that your copilot can be watching the GPS receiver's screen to keep you on course, and can guide you back if you make a wrong turn.

Turn-by-Turn Guidance

If you expect to do much highway navigation using your outdoor-oriented GPS receiver, you should invest in one that offers turn-by-turn guidance capability. The Garmin GPSmap 60CSx and the Magellan eXplorist 500 LE are two good examples. Once loaded with the appropriate software map, either can guide you to a destination along the appropriate roads and highways.

Out of the box, the GPS receiver includes only a high-level base map. To get turn-by-turn guidance, you'll need to install more detailed maps using mapping software purchased from the receiver's manufacturer. Not every program is compatible with every receiver, so refer to the manufacturer's website for specific information. For eXplorist products, Magellan recommends MapSend DirectRoute. For the GPSmap 60CSx, Garmin recommends MapSource City Navigator or City Select. Other programs such as Garmin's

The simplified sequence for navigating to a street address using the GPSmap 60CSx: After pushing the FIND button, choose ADDRESSES (upper left). Enter the address and select the desired choice from the list of matches. After selecting GOTO, choose the FOLLOW ROAD option. The receiver automatically calculates the route and guides you to your destination using text messages displayed on screen (right). Since it doesn't offer voice prompts, navigation is a two-person job.

MapSource MetroGuide will upload similar maps but won't provide turn-by-turn guidance.

Your first task is to get the maps into your receiver. Connect it to the computer using either a USB port or serial port, depending on the model. Launch the software program on your computer and let it detect the GPS receiver. Zoom into the region of interest and click on the map selection tool. Highlight the map regions you want to upload, making sure you don't exceed the receiver's storage limit. (Each time you upload maps, all previous maps are erased, so you always have the full amount of memory available.)

To upload maps using MapSource, you select the "transfer" pull-down menu, then "send to device." With MapSend, you select the "upload regions" button on the toolbar. The time necessary to transfer the files will range from a few minutes for a single region to several hours if you are uploading the entire US onto a 2 gigabyte memory card. Once the files are stored in your receiver, you won't need your computer again until you want to load a different set of maps.

You can select from several navigation options when using the FOLLOW ROAD option on the GPSmap 60CSx.

Navigating to an Address

Once the maps are stored in your receiver, you're ready to navigate. We will use the Garmin GPSmap 60CSx to illustrate how to navigate to a street address.

After turning on your receiver and letting it acquire its position, push the FIND button. You are given a number of choices, including waypoints, geocaches, cities, points of interest, and addresses. Select ADDRESSES and enter the state, city, number, and street of the desired address. A list of matches appears in the display. Select the correct choice, then choose GOTO. You will be asked if you want to FOLLOW ROAD or go OFF ROAD. Select FOLLOW ROAD (OFF ROAD gives you the direct bearing and distance "as the crow flies"). In a few seconds, your receiver calculates the route and gives you the initial driving instruction. To see a complete list of all driving instructions, push the PAGE button.

It's best to keep the map screen displayed as you drive. As you approach a turn, the receiver beeps and provides written instructions for what to do. Have your copilot read the instructions so you can stay focused on driving. Continue following the instructions until you reach your destination.

You can also navigate to any stored waypoint (unlike Internet mapping programs, which require an address). Simply call up the waypoint using the FIND button, select GOTO, and specify FOLLOW ROAD. Note that if the waypoint is not along a road, the software makes a guess as to where you should exit the road. This might not be where you actually want to exit, so use common sense and good judgment when deciding.

When using FOLLOW ROAD with the GPSmap 60CSx, you can select from several routing options. Route choices include fastest time or shortest distance, and the route can be customized depending on whether you are driving a car, bicycle, or truck. You can also choose to avoid certain types of roads. Remember, though, that you still need to exercise common sense to avoid unexpected problems as you navigate.

Other Recommendations

Besides using a copilot, there are a few other practicalities to keep in mind. Your receiver may not pick up satellite signals very well when it's inside an automobile. It will do better when placed on the dashboard where it can "see" through the windshield, rather than inside under the car's metal roof. Don't just lay it on the dashboard though; you'll need to secure it to prevent it from sliding around and becoming a dangerous projectile as you turn. If your receiver can accept an external antenna, consider investing in one. Put the antenna where it has a good view of the sky, and keep the GPS receiver conveniently nearby. Although I've seen some people recommend that the external antenna be magnetically mounted to the outside roof of the car, I've had excellent success attaching it to the rearview mirror by wrapping the cable several times snugly around the mirror support post. Newer GPS units with high-sensitivity receiver chips don't need an external antenna.

Some automobile windshields have metallic coatings that interfere with satellite signal reception. If you can't get your receiver to work anywhere inside your car, this may be your problem. You'll have to use an external antenna attached to the outside roof, with the antenna cable routed through a slightly open window.

Finally, consider investing in an external power cord designed to run your receiver from your car's 12-volt power outlet. You don't want to run your batteries down before you even get to the starting point.

GPS Receiver Selection Guide

This chapter briefly reviews various GPS receivers suitable for outdoor recreational use. Equipment manufacturers are constantly updating their product lines, so before making a purchase decision, visit your local outdoor specialty shop or do research on the Internet to get current information. A good starting point is gpsinformation. net, which covers a wide range of GPS-related subjects. You might also want to watch or join the discussions on the Google GPS newsgroup site at groups.google.com/group/sci.geo.satellite-nav/topics.

The receivers described here were expressly designed for use in the outdoors, and the emphasis is on products for the North American market. This chapter doesn't cover such specialty products as receivers designed to work through a personal computer or PDA, GPS wristwatches, or products intended primarily for marine, aircraft, or automobile use. I strongly believe that if you intend to use GPS in the outdoors, you need a receiver specifically designed for that purpose. While it might be reasonable to use a PDA-based GPS receiver for vehicle navigation, it's a poor tradeoff in the wilderness. You'll make large sacrifices in the unit's ruggedness, water resistance, battery life, and ease of use. As both PDAs and their GPS attachments continue to improve, this might change in the future.

The receivers described here all have at least 12 parallel channels and meet the minimum requirements laid out in Chapter 2. Most will do much more. At a minimum, they can:

▶ Report your position in latitude and longitude or UTM

▶ Select from different map datums, including WGS 84 and NAD 27

▶ Determine your speed and direction of travel

▶ Store at least 500 waypoint locations

▶ Calculate the direction and distance from your current location to any stored waypoint, and from one waypoint to another

► Plot track logs of your journeys

► Withstand at least 30 minutes of immersion in 1 meter of water, per the IEC 529 IPX7 standard

Garmin International Inc.

Garmin (www.garmin.com) is a long-established manufacturer of GPS equipment that offers several product families for the outdoor recreation market, from the diminutive Geko to the full-size GPSMAP 76CSx. You'll find a Garmin receiver for just about every combination of feature set and price point.

GPSmap 60 Family

These flagship products for the outdoor navigator offer an impressive array of features. The two top-end units, the GPSmap 60Cx and 60CSx are mapping receivers with auto-routing capability that include a daylight-viewable color display, built-in base map, 64-megabyte removable microSD memory card (expandable to 2 gigabytes), and full compatibility with most MapSource products. Of particular interest is their use of high-sensitivity receiver technology from SiRF Technology. This delivers a noticeable improvement in the receiver's ability to maintain satellite lock under difficult conditions such as indoors or under heavy tree cover. The "S" in the 60CSx means the receiver includes a built-in barometric altimeter and a true magnetic compass.

The less expensive GPSmap 60 uses a four-level grayscale display and 24-megabyte, built-in memory. It lacks the high-sensitivity SiRF receiver. The low-cost GPS 60 is a nonmapping receiver with 1 megabyte of memory that can be used to store cities and other points of interest.

The well-designed keypad on these receivers includes MARK and FIND buttons as well as a multipurpose, four-direction rocker switch. It is used to enter waypoint coordinates and names, select from various menu choices, and pan th e map display horizontally and vertically.

GPSmap 60CSx (Garmin International)

All products in the GPSmap 60 family use a sensitive quadrifilar helix antenna. They also offer a dedicated geocaching mode that allows you to include hints and log the find for later download to a computer. Battery life is claimed to be as much as 18 hours for products with color displays and 28 hours for those with grayscale displays. They include both an RS-232 serial port and Garmin's proprietary USB interface for high-speed data transfer.

eTrex Family

This is really two separate families with the same name. The eTrex "classic" receivers described here have grayscale displays. The eTrex C products, described next, have color displays and a different user interface in a slightly wider package.

The six products in the classic eTrex family range from the basic yellow eTrex with its bare-minimum feature set to the full-featured Vista. The more expensive members of the family incorporate a thumb-operated joystick (formerly called the "thumb stick") that provides a better user interface than the simple pushbuttons of the more basic products.

The plain, yellow eTrex and its camouflage-colored equivalent are the least expensive members of the family. They don't have internal maps and don't include any additional features like magnetic compasses or barometric altimeters. Their specifications have changed over the years. Those sold today include WAAS capability, but those sold several years ago do not. They can store 500 waypoints, 20 routes, and up to 10 saved tracks. The Camo also offers a few additional features like a hunting/fishing calculator mainly of interest to sportsmen. If you don't mind using paper maps and don't want to spend a lot of money, the basic eTrex is a reasonable choice, but bear in mind you won't be able to upgrade it if you later want more features.

Next lowest in price is the Venture. It adds the thumb stick and a rudimentary mapping capability limited to an internal worldwide city database. The Venture also has the ability to download MapSource points of interest. With only 1 megabyte of internal storage, you can't download road maps or topographic information.

eTrex Venture
(Garmin International)

The Legend, with 8 megabytes of memory, is the least expensive eTrex mapping receiver.

At a list price only slightly more than the Venture, most people find it the better choice.

The Summit takes a different approach. It doesn't accept download-ed maps or points of interest, so it is more like the basic eTrex. What it adds are a barometric altimeter and electronic compass. It can store 20 routes and 10 tracks. Newer versions are WAAS enabled.

The top end of the eTrex line is the Vista. Its 24 megabytes of internal memory is sufficient to store street maps of a small state or topo maps of a large national park. Like the Summit, it includes a separate, electronic compass and a barometric altimeter, and like the Legend, it can store 1000 waypoints, 20 routes, and 10 tracks. It, too, is WAAS compatible.

All eTrex products are small, lightweight, and fairly rugged. The user interface is a bit spartan, with a minimum number of dedicated keys limited to PAGE, ENTER, POWER, and an UP/DOWN rocker switch. Models with the thumb stick are a bit easier to use.

The eTrex receivers use a rectangular patch antenna (you can actu-ally see it through the translucent cases of the Venture and Legend) that isn't quite as sensitive under heavy tree cover as larger receivers such as the GPSmap 60Cx. The internal memory in these receivers is not ac-cessible by the user, so it isn't possible to increase it or swap memory cards. All eTrex receivers can connect to a personal computer through the old RS-232 serial port interface, allowing you to transfer waypoints, routes, and tracks in either direction, and upload MapSource maps to the receiver. As is typical of serial connections, data transfer is fairly slow. Uploading a full 24 megabytes to a Vista takes over an hour.

eTrex Cx Family

Although superficially similar to the eTrex classic family, these three receivers have color displays and are really more like baby ver-sions of the GPSmap 60 family. The Venture Cx has a color display, a slot for an optional microSD memory card, and a built-in base map. With optional City Navigator software, it can provide turn-by-turn guidance to any address you specify (text guidance only, no voice command capability). The Legend Cx includes a 64-megabyte memory card, and the Vista Cx adds a barometric altimeter and magnetic compass. Although they don't use the high-sensitivity SiRF receiver, they do boast a 32-hour battery life. All use Garmin's

eTrex Vista Cx
(Garmin International)

thumb stick, and all connect to a computer via Garmin's proprietary USB interface. The newest models, those with an "H" in the suffix, include a high-sensitivity receiver for better reception in difficult environments.

GPS 76 Family

The products in this family are especially popular for marine applications, but are very suitable for general outdoor use. These units are physically larger than the GPSmap 60 series, but with a similar size display. They have eight dedicated keys and a four-position rocker switch used to make menu selections. All five models are WAAS compatible. They all use quadrifilar helix antennas and include an external antenna connector.

GPSmap 76CSx
(Garmin International)

The basic GPS 76 has a four-level grayscale display and can store 500 waypoints, 50 routes, and 2048 track log points. Its 1 megabyte of internal memory can only be used to store points of interest, not actual maps. The GPSmap 76 increases memory to 8 megabytes and track log points to 10,000. It is compatible with all MapSource products. The GPSmap 76S has 24 megabytes of internal memory and adds a barometric altimeter and magnetic fluxgate compass. The GPSmap 76C includes the high-sensitivity SiRF receiver, a 256-color, daylight-readable display, and 128 megabytes of removable microSD memory. The GPSmap 76Cx adds a barometric altimeter and a magnetic compass.

Products in the GPS 76 family are a good choice for people who want to do a lot of highway or marine navigation in addition to wilderness exploration. The tradeoff is greater size and weight when you're out on a hike. Note that the GPSmap 60Cx and 60CSx have the same size display and are otherwise similar in a slightly smaller package.

Geko Family

The two members of this family are remarkably small and light. They measure in at just under 4 inches high, 2 inches wide, and 1 inch thick. At only 2.3 ounces, they are less than half the weight of an eTrex. The Geko 201 can store 500 waypoints, 20 routes, and 10,000 track log points. It meets what I consider the minimum requirements for general outdoor use. The Geko 301 adds a barometric altimeter and magnetic fluxgate compass. Since neither is a mapping receiver, they are impractical for in-vehicle use. They connect to a computer using the old RS-232 serial port. To achieve their small size, they employ two AAA batteries, giving them nine to 12 hours of useful life per set.

Rino Family

The Rino, an acronym for "Radio Integrated with Navigation for the Outdoors," is a GPS receiver integrated with a two-way radio. There are currently five models, the Rino 110, 120, 130, 520, and 530.

The two-way radio capability in these receivers is unique. Rinos can broadcast on both the free Family Radio Service (FRS) channels and the more powerful General Mobile Radio System (GMRS) frequencies, which require an $85 FCC license. The license is assigned to a specific adult, not a specific radio, and the FCC permits immediate family members of the licensee to use more than one radio to communicate with each other under one license. Non-family members would need separate licenses. (Regulations sometimes change, so make sure you understand current law before using GMRS frequencies.) If you intend to use GMRS frequencies, be sure to purchase this license, as unlicensed use can result in a fine of $10,000 per day. For more information, visit the FCC website at wireless.fcc.gov/services/personal/generalmobile.

The GPS portion of the Rino 110 has 1 megabyte internal memory that can only be used to store points of interest, not complete maps. The Rino 120 increases the internal memory to 8 megabytes and adds full MapSource compatibility. The Rino 130 has 24 megabytes of memory, plus a built-in barometric altimeter and magnetic compass. All models in the 100-series have grayscale displays.

The 500-series Rinos are distinguished by their color displays and more modern GPS capabilities. The Rino 520 has 56 megabytes of internal memory, a USB interface, turn-by-turn auto routing capability, and a more powerful GMRS two-way radio. The Rino 530 adds the barometric altimeter and magnetic compass.

Geko 201
(Garmin International)

Rino 530
(Garmin International)

Canadian law has recently changed and now permits two-way radio transmission on GMRS frequencies, although older Rinos sold in Canada don't include this capability. Unlike the US, Canada does not charge a license fee for use of GMRS frequencies. Outside of Canada and the US, check local laws before using any FRS or GMRS radio, as many countries prohibit their use.

The two-way radio can communicate with any FRS or GMRS radio, so if you already own one, you don't have to buy more than one Rino. If you do, though, you get certain advantages: Two Rinos can transmit and display their positions on each others' map screens, allowing you to track the location and movement of the other person. In the past, the FCC permitted this use only on FRS frequencies, but recent rule changes now allow it on GMRS frequencies. Owners of older Rinos can download a free software update to add this capability.

Lowrance Electronics, Inc.

Lowrance (www.lowrance.com) is well-known for their line of sport fishing SONAR fish finders and their marine and aircraft navigation equipment. The company is also an established player in the recreational outdoor market through its iFinder line of GPS receivers.

iFinder Family

The eight models in this line can be divided into two families: those with grayscale displays and those with color displays. All iFinders currently sold are waterproof to the IPX7 standard, although older units are not. All have built-in base maps and all except the GO and GO2 have external antenna connectors. Models with the "Plus Package" option include the MapCreate software, an MMC card, and a USB card reader.

The basic iFinder GO has a 2-inch grayscale display and 32 megabytes of internal memory preloaded with a US base map that includes marine navigation aids. It can store 1000 waypoints and 100 tracks (called "trails" by Lowrance). Each trail can hold up to 10,000 points. The iFinder GO2 is similar, but with 64 megabytes of built-in memory for a more

iFinder H20c (Courtesy of Lowrance)

detailed US base map. Both have 16-channel receivers for fast acquisition times.

The iFinder H2O, iFinder Hunt, and iFinder Explorer are 12-channel receivers with 3-inch grayscale displays. They have built-in US base maps and slots for optional MMC or SD memory cards to hold more detailed maps. The iFinder Explorer includes a built-in barometric altimeter and a magnetic compass. The iFinder Hunt is basically an Explorer with a customized hunting mode of operation. It also includes a unique voice-recording capability that allows you to attach audible notes to waypoints. All are compatible with Lowrance MapCreate software, as well as their various marine- and lake-mapping software products.

The iFinder H2OC, Hunt C, and Expedition C are 16-channel receivers with color displays. Like their grayscale counterparts, they include built-in US base maps and slots for optional MMC or SD memory cards. They work with Lowrance MapCreate software. The Expedition C includes a barometric altimeter, magnetic compass, and the voice recording capability. It can also play MP3 audio files stored on the MMC card. The Hunt C is like an Expedition C with a slightly smaller screen and the customized hunting mode of operation.

All Lowrance iFinder products have an RS-232 serial port conforming to the NMEA 0183 data transfer standard. This is the dominant standard for the boating industry, which is a strong market for Lowrance. Be aware that the serial port on some iFinders is not designed to interface to a computer, but rather to marine equipment such as autopilots. For units with removable memory, this isn't really a problem because the memory card connects to a computer through a separate SD/MMC high-speed USB card reader.

DeLorme

DeLorme (www.delorme.com) is a major manufacturer of both paper and software topographic and highway maps. Their flagship products are Street Atlas USA and TopoUSA, two well-regarded software programs. Street Atlas USA is a vector graphics map with street-level detail of the USA and Canada. TopoUSA is a vector graphics topo map of the entire US that provides resolution similar to USGS 7.5-minute topo maps.

Earthmate GPS PN-20

In early 2007, DeLorme introduced a handheld GPS receiver, the Earthmate GPS PN-20, designed for the outdoor market. Housed in a yellow and black case, it includes a high-resolution, daylight-viewable, full-color display, 75 megabytes of internal memory, a slot for removable SD memory, a fast USB interface connection, and a user-friendly keypad that includes dedicated MARK and FIND buttons, as well as a four-way rocker switch. The high-sensitivity receiver circuitry from STMicroelectronics includes WAAS capability. The PN-20 can hold up to 1000 waypoints, 10 tracks of 10,000 points each, and 50 routes When loaded with optional mapping software, the PN-20 can give turn-by-turn navigation guidance.

Earthmate GPS PN-20

The PN-20 offers several unique and interesting features. It is compatible with TopoUSA, which is included in your purchase. Besides allowing you to transfer waypoints and tracks, you can also transfer TopoUSA topo maps into the PN-20. In addition, the PN-20 is the only outdoor-oriented GPS receiver that allows you to load aerial photographs and scanned versions of USGS 7.5-minute topo maps for display on the receiver's screen. The aerial photos and USGS topo maps must be purchased from DeLorme by downloading from their website (a limited number of downloads are included free with the receiver). Once loaded, you can quickly switch between the various topographic and photographic views for any location of interest.

DeLorme engineers made a few non-standard choices in the design of the PN-20: First, there is no GOTO command. Instead, you always use the ROUTE command, even for a direct GOTO function. Second, the bearing and distance to your destination do not automatically update as you move. You have to manually ask it to update. Once you get used to them, neither is a problem, and the PN-20 performs similarly to other GPS receivers.

Magellan Navigation, Inc.

Magellan (www.magellangps.com) offers a range of consumer GPS receivers for highway and outdoor navigation, as well as a separate line of professional receivers for the surveying and GIS industries. Its main products for the outdoor market are the eXplorist family and the new Triton family of receivers.

eXplorist Family

This is actually two families with a single name. The models 100 through 600 are a smaller physical size and cover a wide range of features, while the eXplorist XL is physically larger, with a large color display.

The least expensive eXplorist is the model 100. This non-mapping receiver includes most of the basics but not much more. It can show your position in latitude and longitude, UTM, and several other formats. It has all the required map datums, a four-level grayscale display, and WAAS capability. It stores 500 waypoints (called "points of interest")

eXplorist 200

and three track logs of 2000 points each. It doesn't include any type of base map, but the biggest concern for many people is that it doesn't have any way of connecting to a computer. You must enter waypoints from the keypad, and you can't transfer track logs to a computer for later analysis. Its low price point may be attractive to casual users.

The eXplorist 200 adds an 8-megabyte North American base map, and the eXplorist 300 adds a barometric altimeter and magnetic compass. Neither includes the computer interface, so you can't transfer tracks and waypoints or add more map detail.

The eXplorist 210 is similar to the 200, but it includes a USB interface to provide compatibility with Magellan's MapSource software maps. The eXplorist 400 uses a Li-ion rechargeable battery rather than the AA batteries in the less expensive units. It includes the USB port, full Map-Source compatibility, and removable SD memory. The eXplorist 500LE is similar to the 400 but uses a full-color, daylight-viewable display. To keep cost down, it uses AA batteries rather than the Li-ion rechargeable battery pack. The top-of-the-line eXplorist 600 includes the color display, rechargeable Li-ion battery pack, USB port, removable SD memory, and a barometric altimeter and magnetic compass.

Triton Family

As this book was going to press, Magellan introduced a family of receivers aimed at the outdoor navigator. The Triton family offers several unique benefits. They are the first outdoor receivers to work with National Geographic's Topo! and Weekend Explorer mapping software.

This provides the ability to display true USGS 7.5-minute topo maps similar to the Delorme PN-20, but with the added ability to display all five scales of National Geographic maps. Like the PN-20, multiple maps can be layered on a single device, allowing you to load Magellan's topographic maps or marine cartography and National Geographic maps at the same time. All members of the family are waterproof to the IPX7 standard, and the high-end members include a color touch-screen display.

Triton 2000

The Triton 200 is the least expensive family member. This basic unit includes a 2.2-inch QVGA color display, a built-in base map, plus a number of preprogrammed points of interest. The Triton 300 includes 10 megabytes of internal memory for storing additional maps, while the Triton 400 adds an SD card slot for unlimited removable memory. The Triton 500 adds a three-axis electronic compass and barometric altimeter.

The two high-end members of the family are the Triton 1500 and Triton 2000. Both have a larger 2.7-inch QVGA color touch screen, SD card slot, built-in audio voice recorder, and LED flashlight. The Triton 2000 includes a 2 megapixel digital camera, three-axis electronic compass, and barometric altimeter.

Brunton Co.

Brunton (www.brunton.com), a division of Swedish manufacturer Silva Production A.B., is more famous for their excellent line of magnetic compasses, capped by the hallmark Brunton Pocket Transit. They were first to offer a consumer GPS receiver with built-in magnetic compass, the Multi-Navigator MNS. Their current product is the Atlas GPS, which is a Lowrance iFinder branded with the Brunton label. It comes in two versions, the basic Atlas and the Atlas MNS, which is like the iFinder Explorer. Both are compatible with MapCreate and Brunton's own TopoCreate software.

GPS Accessories

There are only a few GPS accessories I consider essential. Most important, in my opinion, is a sturdy case. GPS receivers are delicate pieces of electronic equipment, so when you are out in the wilderness, they need as much protection as possible. You can use generic cases designed for

Computer screen displays of Yosemite Valley as shown by two MapSource products: Roads and Recreation (above) and Topo (below). Either map can be loaded into Garmin's mapping receivers.

compact digital cameras or a custom case specifically designed for your receiver. I like the hard-sided cases from AccuCase (www.accucase. com), which are compact and lightweight but also provide solid protection. They offer several custom GPS cases, including dedicated cases for the Garmin eTrex, Geko, and III+, and a more generic case for various Magellan and Garmin receivers.

If you own a mapping receiver, you'll probably want to invest in the appropriate software mapping program from your receiver's manufacturer. That way, you can load more detailed maps than available from the built-in base map, limited only by the amount of receiver memory.

Both Garmin (MapSource) and Magellan (MapSend) offer several alternatives, depending on your needs. You can choose from topographic, highway, or marine maps. With the right receiver, a highway map can guide you to an exact street address. Topo maps are great for the outdoor adventurer but can't automatically guide you to a destination. Since they are based on USGS topo maps, their road detail is not as current as a true highway-mapping program. If you buy a topo program, make sure you know the level of detail you are getting. Some programs provide the equivalent of 1:100,000 paper maps, while a few offer detail similar to a 1:24,000 USGS 7.5-minute map. The opposite page compares the detail of Yosemite Valley shown by Garmin's MapSource Topo program with the same area shown by their Roads and Recreation program.

DeLorme's PN-20 is compatible with TopoUSA software. It also offers the unique ability to download aerial photographs and scanned copies of USGS topo maps from the DeLorme website. When all three are loaded into the receiver, you can quickly switch between different displays.

Lowrance and Brunton both use the MapCreate software (called TopoCreate by Brunton), which combines highway, topographic, and marine databases. Both also offer maps pre-loaded on MMC cards. This is particularly convenient for extended trips where you can't easily upload new maps from a computer to your receiver as you travel.

To connect your receiver to a personal computer, you'll need the appropriate interface cable. Newer receivers use standard USB cables, but older receivers use RS-232 serial cables. These are custom designs, so your best bet is to purchase the cable offered by your receiver's manufacturer. You can sometimes save money by purchasing a third-party cable off the Internet, but the quality of such products varies widely.

Another useful cable is one that lets you connect your receiver to an automobile cigarette lighter socket. If you intend to use your receiver in a vehicle, you won't want to depend on battery power. Again, this is a custom-designed cable best purchased from the manufacturer of your receiver. You may also need to use this cable if you want to run your receiver from a 110-volt outlet. Most receivers don't offer a convenient way to plug into AC power, so if this is important you may need to purchase an adapter that converts 110 volts AC to 12 volts DC through a cigarette lighter socket. Then plug your automobile adapter into this socket.

Finally, an Internet search on the words "GPS accessories" will yield an almost unlimited range of products of varying usefulness. Depending on your intended use, you might choose to invest in such accessories as a bicycle handlebar mount, external antenna, PDA interface cable, automobile mount, training video, rechargeable batteries, or a wide variety of other software products.

If you use your GPS receiver in the outdoors, you need a sturdy case. This hard-shell case made by AccuCase is specifically designed for the Garmin eTrex series.

Appendix I

GPS FAQs

These days, lists of frequently asked questions, or FAQs, are all the rage. It would seem incomplete to offer a book on GPS navigation that doesn't include some sort of FAQ list, so here it is. Many of these topics have already been covered elsewhere in the book, but they are conveniently collected here in one place for easy reference. Some of the topics, ones of general interest but not essential for outdoor navigators, are covered here for the first time.

My GPS instruction manual makes it sound like I only need to track three satellites to find my position. You say I need four. What's the story?

To *accurately* find your position, you need to be tracking four satellites. This is something many GPS instruction manuals don't explain very well. They might say something like, "With three satellites, your receiver does not report elevation." This makes it sound like your horizontal position is still reported accurately. This is not necessarily the case. To get good results, your receiver needs accurate elevation information. The fourth satellite gives it the ability to make that calculation. Without a fourth satellite, it must assume an elevation. The only one it knows is the last one it measured, but if you've changed position since then, your actual elevation could be considerably different. This can result in errors of a mile or more from your true position. When it is critical that you know your exact position, don't believe your GPS receiver unless it is tracking at least four satellites.

Is my GPS receiver's readout of speed very accurate?

Yes, it is quite accurate, even better than the speedometer in your car. Contrary to what many people think, your receiver does not measure speed by calculating how fast your position changes. If it did, it would be much less accurate. It actually calculates speed by measuring the Doppler shifts of the satellite signals. It's the same principle that police radar guns use to determine how fast a car is traveling, and it has similar accuracy.

How accurately can my GPS receiver find my position?

Unfortunately, that's not an easy question to answer. It depends on several factors, some in your control, others not. The number of satellites being tracked and their locations in the sky are very important. Ideally, you want to be tracking one satellite overhead and three more spaced equally around you midway up from the horizon. Four satellites in a straight line is the worst configuration. Other error sources include atmospheric effects and the current level of solar activity (such things as sunspots and solar flares).

It's safe to assume that when locked on to at least four satellites, your GPS receiver can find its position to within about 50 feet. Most of the time, it will be much better, approaching 25 feet or less. On rare occasions, it may be worse. It is not possible to reliably achieve accuracies in the range of 10 feet or less without WAAS or DGPS. And yes, the more satellites you are tracking, the better the accuracy.

Does GPS work underwater?

No. Even an inch of water is enough to completely block the satellite signals and prevent your receiver from finding its position. Receivers are designed to be waterproof so they won't get damaged if you use them in the rain or if they accidentally get dunked in a lake or river. They can not find your position underwater.

What about rain and clouds? Don't they also block the satellite signals?

No, water vapor or isolated droplets don't have much of an effect on the satellite signals (for the engineers in the crowd, the attenuation is less than 2 dB). The only thing you might have to worry about is if your receiver's antenna gets completely coated with water as a result of heavy rain. But in that case, you can just wipe the water away and solve the problem.

Why does my receiver lose satellite lock under heavy tree cover?

Tree leaves are full of water. It's like having a solid film of water between you and the satellites. Depending on its design, a receiver may be more or less sensitive to this effect. A receiver with a good, high-gain antenna and low-noise electronics will do somewhat better than a receiver with a smaller antenna and less expensive circuitry. But no receiver will work well under heavy tree cover.

How accurate is my receiver as an altimeter?

The GPS readout of altitude is not very accurate, despite what you may read in Internet chat groups. Several factors come into play: First, the

GPS system wasn't designed to measure altitude (called "elevation" in GPS language) accurately. The problem comes in the design of the satellite orbits. The details are fairly technical, but simply stated, the orbits are well-designed for measuring horizontal positions, not for vertical positions. The vertical measurement uncertainty is about three times worse than horizontal uncertainty.

Another problem comes from how elevation is defined: Topo maps and elevation signs report altitude referenced to mean sea level. Your GPS receiver measures it against a mathematical model of the earth. This model can be tens of feet different from true mean sea level in some areas. Overall, you can't expect a GPS receiver to measure elevation to better than a few hundred feet accuracy, and in some cases it can be much worse. If you want to accurately measure elevation, you must use a calibrated barometric altimeter. Some more expensive receivers include a separate barometric altimeter just for this purpose.

How good is my GPS receiver as a compass?

That's a trick question. A GPS receiver doesn't really function as a true compass. Its "compass" page is actually an indicator that shows what direction you are *moving*, not what direction it is *pointed*. If you stop moving, it stops working. It is really a heading indicator, not a compass. When you are moving faster than about 10 miles per hour, it does a very good job. Below that speed, electrical noise and system inaccuracies introduce more errors. It is still pretty good, though. I've never had a problem using the compass page to guide me to a hidden geocache, as long as I keep moving.

Some GPS receivers have a separate, built-in electronic compass. This is a true magnetic compass that is entirely separate from the GPS functionality. These types of compasses can find a bearing to an accuracy of 5 degrees or less, similar to an ordinary baseplate compass. It's an expensive addition to your receiver and it eats up batteries rapidly, so you should still carry a separate baseplate compass.

Will my GPS receiver work inside a commercial aircraft?

It's possible. You need to be sitting at a window seat with your receiver pressed right up against the window. If you're lucky, the satellites will be in exactly the right positions, and you can lock onto at least a few. (Even 2D mode is useful here since a mile or two error in location will still give you a good idea of where you are.)

It may take a lot longer for your receiver to get a position fix because you are traveling in the neighborhood of 600 miles per hour. (You'll see your exact speed when your receiver is locked on.)

A more important question is whether you are even allowed to operate a GPS receiver inside an aircraft. As of this writing, there are no laws prohibiting the use of GPS receivers in the US, so it is strictly up to the individual airlines. Some airlines allow you to do so after the aircraft has reached cruising altitude, while others prohibit it at all times. None allows you to operate it during the critical takeoff and landing phases. Check gpsinformation.net for a current listing of various airline policies.

Does my GPS receiver send out a signal the government or anyone else can use to track my location?

No. GPS is a completely passive system. You can receive signals from the satellites, but your receiver is not a transmitter. It doesn't broadcast any kind of information about your position. Like almost all electronics, though, it does emit very low levels of radio waves that could theoretically interfere with the operation of sensitive equipment nearby. That is why airlines won't let you use a GPS receiver (or any other electronic device) during takeoff or landing.

How is a route different from a track?

A route is something you create and enter into your receiver. It is a collection of waypoints you have organized into a specific sequence. When navigating a route, your receiver guides you from one waypoint to the next in sequence. When you arrive at one waypoint, it automatically switches to guide you to the next one. Your receiver can only show you the straight-line path from one waypoint to the next.

A track is not something you manually enter. It is a detailed record of the exact path you have been following. When you activate the tracking function, your GPS receiver automatically plots track points at regular intervals to map your path. There may be hundreds or thousands of points on a track, but they are not named waypoints and you can't easily read latitudes and longitudes of track points like you can for waypoints.

What is the "track back" function?

Many receivers offer a way to easily reverse your outbound track and follow it back to its origin. In this mode, your receiver automatically creates a route from its stored track. This can be useful if you need to closely follow your exact path back to where you started. This "track back" route creates a series of phantom waypoints along your original track that lets you return along your original route. Since a "track back" route consists of only a limited number of waypoints, it will not include all the detail of the original track.

Why does my receiver sometimes report fantastic speeds of many hundreds of miles per hour or show large, rapid variations in my position, even when I am standing still?

This is the result of a problem called multipath error. You'll usually see this in difficult terrain like canyons, mountainous regions, or heavy tree cover, and in cities with numerous tall buildings. Your GPS receiver determines its position by measuring the time it takes for a radio signal to travel from a satellite to the receiver. This assumes the signal traveled in a straight line the whole time. Objects like mountains or skyscrapers can reflect the signal and make it appear to take a longer time to reach the receiver. If your receiver is picking up both the straight line and reflected signal, it can get confused and think you are moving very rapidly.

Why does my GPS receiver sometimes take a long time to find its position and at other times do so very quickly?

Your receiver needs two types of data to find its position: First, it must have a valid almanac that indicates the general locations of every satellite in the sky. Second, it must have valid ephemeris data for each satellite it is tracking. This is the very accurate information on a satellite's orbit that your receiver uses to calculate its position.

Almanac data remains valid for about six months. As long as you use your receiver more often than that, it doesn't have to load a new almanac. If you let the almanac get stale, your receiver will need 10 to 20 minutes to load a new almanac.

Ephemeris data remains valid for only a few hours. It should take only a minute or so to load new ephemeris data from a satellite, and it can do this for all satellites at once. Since it might not start tracking all satellites at the same time, it could take a couple of minutes to load all the ephemeris information and find its position.

If you have used your receiver in the last hour or two, both almanac and ephemeris data should be valid, so your receiver can often find its position in only a few seconds.

If your receiver loses track of a satellite at any time while it is loading ephemeris data, it has to start over again. So if you travel under trees or drive under a bridge while your receiver is attempting to find its position, it can take a long time to lock on.

Can I load third-party software maps into my mapping receiver?

For the most part, if you want to display maps on your screen, you must buy the software from your receiver's manufacturer. Third-party software mapping programs such as National Geographic's Topo! or

Maptech's Terrain Navigator are designed to work with GPS receivers by transferring waypoints, routes, and tracks to your receiver and back, but they do not transfer the maps themselves. (Magellan's Triton series is an exception; they work specifically with National Geographic's maps.) If you search the Internet, you may read about creative hackers who claim to have gotten around this limitation, but that's not something the average user should consider doing.

What are the best batteries to use in my receiver?

Most receiver manufacturers recommend alkaline batteries as the best overall choice. Alkalines give good life and are relatively inexpensive. These are the batteries receiver manufacturers use to measure battery life.

Cost- and environmental-conscious people sometimes use nickel metal-hydride (NiMH) rechargeable batteries. These are initially more expensive than alkalines, but they can be recharged hundreds of times. High-power NiMH batteries rated at 2000 mAh or higher can last on a single charge nearly as long as alkalines. Like all rechargeables, they discharge fairly rapidly, even when not being used, losing as much as half their charge in just a few weeks, so don't use NiMH batteries in critical situations.

Nickel-cadmium (NiCad) batteries are another type of rechargeable battery that has been around longer than NiMH. They don't last as long on a single charge, and since cadmium is a toxic metal that is subject to increasing environmental regulations, they are being phased out in favor of NiMH.

Lithium batteries are expensive and not rechargeable (except for custom Li-ion battery packs supplied with some receivers), but they can be useful in certain instances. They last about 30 percent longer than alkalines, but their real value is in cold weather. While other batteries quickly lose efficiency as the temperature approaches freezing, lithium batteries do a much better job of maintaining power. Here is a very rough comparison of the performance of different battery types:

Type	Relative Life Per Charge	Cost	Rechargeable?
Lithium	130%	High	No
Alkaline	100%	Low	No
NiMH	60-100%	Highest	Yes
NiCad	25-35%	Medium	Yes

Appendix II

Resources

Books

Kals, W.S. with Clyde Soles. *Land Navigation Handbook: The Sierra Club Guide to Map, Compass, and GPS*. San Francisco: Sierra Club Books, 2005.

Beffort, Brian. *Joy of Backpacking*. Berkeley, CA: Wilderness Press, 2007.

Jordan, Ryan, Ed. *Lightweight Backpacking and Camping*. Berkeley, CA: Wilderness Press, 2005.

Manning, Harvey. *Backpacking One Step at a Time*. New York: Vintage Books, 1986.

Ferguson, Michael. *GPS Land Navigation*. Boise, Idaho: Glassford Publishing, 1997.

Equipment Manufacturers

Brunton: www.brunton.com
DeLorme: www.delorme.com
Garmin: www.garmin.com
Lowrance: www.lowrance.com
Magellan: www.magellangps.com

Maps

www.fugawi.com/web
maps.google.com
www.maptech.com
maps.nationalgeographic.com/topo
www.oziexplorer.com

www.topozone.com
www.usgs.gov

General GPS Information

www.gpsinformation.net
www.thespacereview.com/article/626/1
gps.faa.gov
www.ngs.noaa.gov/GEOID

Geocaching

www.geocaching.com
www.navicache.com
brillig.com/geocaching
www.geocacher-u.com
geocaching.gpsgames.org

Land Navigation Practices

www.globalsecurity.org/military/library/policy
/army/fm/3-25-26

Glossary

2D mode The mode of operation of a GPS receiver in which it is tracking only three satellites. Positions calculated while a receiver is in 2D mode can be subject to large uncertainties and should never be relied on when navigating in the outdoors.

2drms Twice distance root-mean-square. A measure of the accuracy of a GPS receiver based on the probability that the position reported by the receiver will be better than the stated number at least 95 percent of the time. Simple rms accuracy is similar but based on a 67 percent probability.

3D mode The mode of operation of a GPS receiver in which it is tracking at least four satellites and can accurately determine its position.

agonic line The line from the North Pole to the South Pole, along which magnetic declination is zero. In the US, the agonic line runs from northeastern Minnesota to the Florida panhandle.

almanac A table of approximate satellite orbital information stored in a GPS receiver and used to predict which satellites should be above the local horizon.

baseplate compass A magnetic compass consisting of a circular vial containing a magnetic needle affixed to transparent base. This is the preferred style of compass for general outdoor navigation.

bearing The direction from your current position to your intended destination. Also known as an azimuth.

bread-crumb trail See "track log."

CEP Circular Error Probable. A measure of the accuracy of a GPS receiver based on a probability that the position reported by the receiver will be better than the CEP 50 percent of the time.

cold start   The process a GPS receiver must perform to find its position when it has a valid almanac but no valid ephemeris data. (Note: Some older texts define cold start as being when your receiver has neither a valid almanac nor valid ephemeris data, but this definition has now fallen out of favor.)

coordinates   The alphanumeric description of a geographic location on earth. The most common coordinate systems are latitude/longitude and UTM, but a GPS receiver can be configured for many other choices as well.

datum   A model of the earth that describes it as an ellipsoid with a fixed origin and major and minor axes of specified lengths. The two most important datums in the US are known as NAD 27 and WGS 84. Strictly speaking, this is known as a horizontal datum, as opposed to a vertical datum, which is used as an elevation reference.

declination   See "magnetic declination."

Differential GPS   A method that uses accurately surveyed base stations and a separate transmitter to correct for GPS errors due to atmospheric distortion. The US Coast Guard operates the most extensive DGPS system, but similar systems are operated on smaller scales by private companies.

DOD   United States Department of Defense. Operates the Global Positioning System.

EPE   Estimated Position Error. Some GPS receivers report this as an approximate indication of the accuracy of the current displayed position.

ephemeris   The very accurate satellite orbital information a GPS receiver uses to calculate its precise distance from the satellite.

fluxgate compass   An electronic version of the traditional magnetic compass.

geocaching   A GPS sport in which one person hides a cache and posts the coordinates on a website. Other people use GPS receivers to locate the cache and exchange items in it.

geocoin   A custom token created by geocachers and placed in a geocache.

geoid   The line of constant gravity that represents mean sea level.

geostationary orbit	A satellite in orbit 22,240 miles above the earth and directly over the equator. At that altitude, the satellite orbits the earth once in 24 hours—the same time it take the earth to complete one rotation. So to a person on earth, a geostationary satellite appears to remain fixed in the sky.
GPS	Global Positioning System.
GPSr	Slang term for GPS receiver.
heading	The direction you are currently moving.
hot start	The process a GPS receiver performs to find its position when it has both a valid almanac and valid ephemeris data for at least four satellites.
initialization	The process employed by a GPS receiver to update its almanac for the current time, satellite orbits, and geographic position when the almanac data is not valid or you have moved more than a few hundred miles from your last position.
ionosphere	The upper atmosphere of the earth, ranging from about 50 miles to 300 miles above the earth's surface. Ionized particles in the ionosphere cause a significant GPS measurement uncertainty that varies greatly depending on time of day and level of solar activity.
LAAS	Local Area Augmentation System. A system designed to improve GPS accuracy in the vicinity of major airports to aid aircraft during instrument landings.
latitude	A line drawn parallel to the equator that measures how far north or south of the equator you are.
longitude	A line drawn from the North Pole to the South Pole that indicates how far east or west of the prime meridian you are.
magnetic declination	For a given location, the difference in direction between true north and magnetic north. Also called magnetic variation.
magnetic north	The direction a magnetic compass points. A physical location in northern Canada near Baffin Island.
MB	Megabytes. A measure of the amount of memory in an electronic device such as a GPS receiver.
meridians	Lines of longitude.
MGRS	Military Grid Reference System. A version of the UTM coordinate system.

multipath   A GPS error that occurs when a satellite signal arrives at the GPS receiver from more than one path, typically because it has been reflected from a large surface such as a metal building or canyon wall. Because the two signals arrive at different times, the receiver can't easily tell which to use to measure the satellite's distance from the receiver.

Navstar   "Navstar Global Positioning System" was the original name given to GPS by the US Department of Defense. While it still shows up on DOD documents, everyone else just calls it "GPS."

neatlines   The borders of a topographic map.

NMEA 0183   An industry standard for communicating between a GPS receiver and other electronic equipment developed by the National Marine Electronics Association.

parallels   Lines of latitude.

planimetric map   The kind of highway maps sold at supermarkets and auto clubs. Planimetric maps don't indicate the nature of the terrain in any detail.

position fix   The process a GPS receiver uses to calculate its geographic position on earth.

prime meridian   The position of 0° longitude. It is a line running from the North Pole to the South Pole through the Royal Observatory at Greenwich, England.

PRN code   Pseudo-random noise code. The binary sequence transmitted by the satellites and used by a GPS receiver to determine the time delay between when the signal was broadcast by the satellite and when it was received by the GPS receiver.

raster-graphics map   A software map derived from the scanned image of a paper map.

route   A series of waypoints stored in a GPS receiver in sequential order. When the route is activated, the GPS receiver guides you from one waypoint to the next in sequence.

Selective Availability   The method once used by the military to artificially degrade the accuracy of civilian GPS. Discontinued by presidential order since May 2, 2000.

SIS   Signal-in-Space. Term used by the Department of Defense to describe the accuracy of the GPS signal as broadcast by the satellites and prior to propagation through the atmosphere.

topographic map	A kind of map that not only shows highways and artificial features, but also uses contour lines to indicate the shape of the terrain.
track log	The digitized record of your exact path of travel as stored by a GPS receiver.
travel bug	A geocache item intended to travel from cache to cache. Travel bugs can be identified by a bar-coded metal tag attached to them.
triangulation	The method used by GPS to determine position. Also the method for determining your position on a map by plotting the intersection of compass bearings to objects in the landscape.
troposphere	The portion of the atmosphere closest to the ground. GPS error introduced within the troposphere is relatively small and predictable.
true north	The direction toward the true North Pole, the axis of the earth's rotation.
USB	Universal Serial Bus. A relatively high-speed interface between a personal computer and a peripheral such as a printer or GPS receiver.
UTM	Universal Transverse Mercator. A rectangular grid used as an alternative to latitude and longitude to describe a position on the surface of the earth.
vector-graphics map	A software map in which features such as roads, rivers, and topographic contours are stored as digital lines.
WAAS	Wide Area Augmentation System. An enhancement to civilian GPS that employs additional satellites and base stations to measure atmospheric distortions and broadcast correction factors that a WAAS-enabled GPS receiver can use to improve accuracy.
warm start	The process a GPS receiver must perform to find its position when it has a valid almanac but only has valid ephemeris data for three satellites.
waypoint	A description of the geographic coordinates of a particular location on earth, named and stored in the memory of a GPS receiver.

Index

About the Author

Steve Hinch has taught courses in GPS navigation to police and fire personnel, park rangers, search-and-rescue staff, and recreational outdoor enthusiasts since 1998. Born in Seattle, he grew up in the Southern California coastal city of Redondo Beach. When Steve was young, his avid rockhound parents would pack up the family and head out to remote desert locations in search of semi-precious stones nearly every weekend. These desert explorations honed his navigation skills and taught him the importance of not getting lost.

Trained as an electrical engineer, Steve has more than 25 years of management experience in the high-technology industry. He holds three patents and has authored three books. He earned BS and Master of Engineering degrees from Harvey Mudd College in Claremont, California. Steve has two grown children and lives with his wife in the heart of the wine country in Santa Rosa, California. He is also an award-winning photographer who specializes in landscapes of the Southwest.